DISCIPLESHIP

Dan Solis

Pacific Press®
Publishing Association
Nampa, Idaho | Oshawa, Ontario, Canada
www.pacificpress.com

Cover design by Gerald Lee Monks
Cover design resources from Lars Justinen
Inside design by Kristin Hansen-Mellish

Copyright © 2013 by Pacific Press® Publishing Association
Printed in the United States of America
All rights reserved

The author assumes full responsibility for the accuracy of all facts and quotations as cited in this book.

Additional copies of this book are available by calling toll-free 1-800-765-6955 or by visiting http://www.adventistbookcenter.com.

Library of Congress Cataloging-in-Publication Data:

Solis, Dan, 1956–
  Discipleship / Dan Solis.
    pages cm
  ISBN 13: 978-0-8163-4522-9 (pbk.)
  ISBN 10: 0-8163-4522-8 (pbk.)
  1. Christian life—Seventh-day Adventist authors. 2. Discipling (Christianity) I. Title.
  BV4501.3.S6576 2013
  248.4'86732—dc23
                          2013022732

13 14 15 16 17 • 5 4 3 2 1

Contents

CHAPTER 1

On July 5, 2009, unemployed coffin maker Terry Herbert took a second-hand metal detector, which he had purchased for £2.5 [US$6] at a garage sale, to Fred Johnson's farm. What the discarded detector uncovered made both men millionaires overnight. The Staffordshire Hoard, as the collection is known, consisted of about thirty-five hundred precious metal artifacts that had been buried, apparently, since the seventh or eighth century. Archaeologists speculate that the gold and silver pieces were likely royal property, essentially military armament. Dating from the time of the Mercian kingdom, the collection was valued at £3.285 million [US$5.5 million]. Besides enriching Herbert and Johnson, the collection has enriched thousands culturally since being displayed at the Birmingham Museum & Art Gallery and at the British Museum. Significantly, the collection includes a gold inscription from the Latin text for Numbers 10:35, which reads, "Rise up, LORD; let Your enemies be scattered, and those who hate You flee before You."

When Jesus came to the earth, He encountered spiritually impoverished people who, ironically, trampled upon even greater treasure. That treasure, however, was buried beneath layers of human misunderstanding and tradition. God's chosen people were close but still far from the knowledge that could release them from spiritual poverty. For centuries, the priceless worth of divine revelation through Scripture was largely forgotten, ignored, or diminished.

Who would have guessed that a Carpenter born inside an animal stable would be God's selected instrument to unearth this priceless treasure! Jesus would scatter the enemies of light and banish sin with its consequences forever. Isaiah looked forward to this day, saying in words Christ would later apply to Himself,

> The Spirit of the Lord GOD is upon Me,
> Because the LORD has anointed Me
> To preach good tidings to the poor;
> He has sent Me to heal the brokenhearted,
> To proclaim liberty to captives,
> And the opening of the prison to those who are bound (Isaiah 61:1).

As Jesus attracted people to Himself, He found that Holy Scripture was an invaluable ally in the cause of making disciples. If new birth and spiritual transformation were going to take place, the scriptural treasure of His time, now commonly called the Old Testament, would play a significant role. Jesus said, "You search the Scriptures because you think they give you eternal life. But the Scriptures point to me! Yet you refuse to come to me to receive this life" (John 5:39, 40, NLT).

The reasoning is simple but profound: Life is found in Jesus, and Jesus is found in Scripture. Those who seek life will find it in God's self-revelation, the Bible. Jesus Himself embodied Scripture.

First, He was born into a home where Scripture was treasured and its instructions followed. Luke records at Jesus' birth, "After doing everything the Lord's Teachings required, Joseph and Mary returned to their hometown of Nazareth in Galilee" (Luke 2:39, GOD'S WORD). In the same chapter, Luke recalls an incident when Jesus was separated from His family while returning home from the annual Passover observance. Thinking that Jesus was with friends and relatives, Joseph and Mary traveled a day without him. Becoming concerned, they inquired of those relatives and friends, but Jesus was not found among them. Anxiously they returned to Jerusalem. "Three days later, they finally discovered him in the Temple, sitting among the religious teachers, listening to them and asking questions. All who heard him were amazed at his understanding and his answers" (verses 46, 47, NLT). How many twelve-year-olds elicit such a description? The nation's religious leaders were amazed by His spiritual understanding. This certainly suggests that Mary and Joseph conscientiously followed the instructions of Deuteronomy 6:

> "You shall love the LORD your God with all your heart, and with all your soul, and with all your might. Keep these words that I am commanding you today in your heart. Recite them to your children and talk about them when you are at home and when you are away, when you lie down and when you rise" (verses 5–7, NRSV).

(In chapter 4, we will explore the importance of cultivating discipleship among children in more depth.)

Second, Christ's dependence upon Scripture is illustrated through His encounter with Satan in the wilderness. Weakened by forty days of fasting, intent on accomplishing the mission His heavenly Father has outlined for Him, Jesus faces off with a cunningly persuasive Satan. Three times he assails Jesus with temptations and three times Jesus responds, "The Scriptures say."

Broad scriptural knowledge was embedded within Christ's thinking. In His humanity, He had memorized copious amounts of the Holy Writings, which He had inspired as God. One day, after His resurrection, He was traveling along the road toward Emmaus and joined two sober-faced disciples so engulfed by their grief that they failed to recognize Him. Hope that the Messiah would establish Himself and His kingdom had disappeared from their minds amid the embarrassment and disappointment of Jesus' crucifixion. The despondent disciples shared their feelings with their unrecognized fellow Traveler, surprised that He was apparently unaware of these recent events. Luke records, "Then Jesus took them through the writings of Moses and *all* the prophets, explaining from *all* the Scriptures the things concerning himself" (Luke 24:27, NLT; emphasis added). Later that evening, they exclaimed to each other, "Didn't our hearts burn within us as he talked with us on the road and explained the Scriptures to us?" (verse 32, NLT).

Christians who conscientiously answer God's call to disciple-making will likewise conscientiously accept God's invitation to scriptural immersion. I tenderly remember a phone conversation with my eighty-nine-year-old father when he joyfully shared that he was completing his first cover-to-cover reading of Scripture. I was actually surprised because I remembered watching him read the Bible often during my childhood and had assumed that he had read it through many times.

My mother and father's influence—specifically through their reading of Scripture—guided my personal spiritual journey. I had attended Christian schools until I entered public high school. There my Vacation Bible School faith slammed against the bastion of scientific opinion. "God" was unneeded, except by weak-minded individuals who needed crutches to handle reality. The "Creator" was a figment of imagination developed through primitive superstitions to explain phenomena now better explicated by modern scientific hypotheses. Almost ready to abandon those "childish religious convictions," I paused to reconsider surrendering my childhood faith—primarily because I recognized that my parents had discovered meaning, purpose, and a hope-filled lifestyle through Scripture's message.

One evening I reached for God, praying, "God, if You really exist, make yourself plain to me and show me what gives life purpose. Whatever that is, I'll put my life into telling others about that." That night I began reading my Bible and charting my progress on the Bible's flyleaf each night. Some nights I'd read several chapters; other times, a handful of verses. Challenged by understanding seventeenth-century English language and a general ignorance of biblical customs, I could not understand many things that I had read. God's Spirit, however, ignited a spiritual fire within me that burns even now, as Scripture yielded the message of God's love and compassionate forgiveness. My parent's example of scriptural immersion had preserved me for God's kingdom.

The vintage King James Version that initiated my Bible reading has long since fallen apart. My library now houses more than thirty-five Scripture translations. Yet I refuse to discard that book because of the personal transformation that God inaugurated through its pages. (Perhaps if this book sells enough copies the royalties will provide enough to have it re-bound!) While the pages have yellowed and disintegrated, my scriptural reading habit has not. Because of my personal inclination toward sinfulness, I usually read the Bible through two to eight times annually. Biblical influence has been the only thing capable of restraining me from plunging headlong into wickedness. "I have hidden your word in my heart that I might not sin against you" (Psalm 119:11, NIV).

The main point is that disciple-makers must first be immersed in Scripture themselves before employing Scripture evangelistically. Proving points and arguing propositions with biblical texts does not require scriptural immersion. Internet access to doctrinal Web sites can accomplish that. Remember, the purpose of scriptural immersion is not bludgeoning religious opponents; the purpose is spiritual transformation.

Obviously, Jesus provides the supreme example. While His discourse effectively corrected doctrinal aberrations, His central purpose was *not* winning arguments. Rather, it was spiritual renewal. Unless the disciple-maker is personally undergoing this spiritual renewal he or she cannot effectively guide people into the kingdom. Likewise, member recruitment does not require scriptural immersion. Worldly enticements for religious affiliation abound. (One church offered a weekly drawing for a microwave oven just for visiting. Perhaps they should raise the ante—monthly drawings for luxury automobiles just for joining.) Nevertheless, genuine conversion will always be associated with scriptural immersion. Those who would be disciple-makers like Christ must first drink deeply from the scriptural fountain. Only then, empowered by divine inspiration, will they effectively lead others into authentic discipleship.

Perhaps some guidelines and benchmarks will be helpful in assisting readers with self-assessment. Because these questions will not necessarily be discussed with other people, complete honesty is encouraged. What proportion of your daily schedule is devoted to scriptural immersion? Include time spent reading and memorizing Scripture, listening to Scripture readings and songs (not merely popular religious music), and singing or meditating upon Scripture. Avoid exaggerating the amount by recording the time actually spent performing these activities during a given week. Compare that amount with the time spent with leisure activities such as surfing the Internet, watching television, listening to the radio or recordings, exercising, texting, social networking, that is, "Facebooking," and participating in group sports.

Do your scripturally oriented activities equal or exceed your leisure activities? Remember, if your daily Scripture exposure equals the textual basis for someone else's daily devotional thought, your total daily scriptural input, morning and evening, probably totals fewer than sixty seconds. Should your daily eating time be limited to sixty seconds, how soon would you collapse? Even reading worthwhile Christian literature (I hope that this book qualifies!) should not be substituted for Scripture reading. If reading *this* book displaces your Scripture-reading time, stop reading immediately. Proceed directly to Scripture and return only after ingesting significant portions of divine revelation. (Please, however, avoid returning this book to your Christian bookstore.)

Your self-evaluation may encourage some lifestyle decisions that your willpower is helpless to effect. You may feel defenseless against self-centered inclinations, lifelong practices, and entrenched habits. Even practices not inherently sinful become impediments to spiritual growth whenever they displace thoughtful time spent with Scripture.

Nevertheless, you are neither hopeless nor helpless. Your heavenly Father, your Eternal Savior, and your Divine Counselor, have willingly placed Themselves and Their spiritual authority at your disposal. Their indomitable strength is perfected in your weakness. Paul wrote, "We have this treasure in clay jars, so that it may be made clear that this extraordinary power belongs to God and does not come from us" (2 Corinthians 4:7, NRSV).

Are you scripturally dehydrated, longing for a spiritually drenching downpour? Are you starving for scriptural nourishment but imprisoned by television, the Internet, or other addictions? Do not misunderstand; this is *not* an oblique reference to pornography, although that is certainly included. I struggle with a fascination of worldwide news, which left unchecked can absorb countless hours, effectively displacing my Scripture-reading time. God, however, can order our priorities whenever we willingly invite His complete and absolute control. This is our primary step in appropriating Scripture in the disciple-making enterprise.

Jesus was permeated by the scriptural message. He embodied holiness, compassion, forgiveness, gentleness, righteousness, faithfulness, and love. The Messiah's character so distinguished Him that Matthew observed, "When Jesus had finished this discourse the people were astounded at his teaching; unlike their own teachers he taught with a note of authority" (Matthew 7:28, 29, NEB). Jesus spoke authoritatively because His message originated from who He was rather than from what others thought. Christ embodied the spiritual transformation that He offered His listeners. He lived Scripture; His antagonists merely debated it. Whenever would-be disciple-makers utilize Scripture argumentatively, like some doctrinal whip, they effectively sacrifice their spiritual authority. Whenever Scripture effectively transforms human lives, permeating them with righteousness, faithfulness, and compassion, those lives become spiritual magnets drawing additional disciples into Christ's family.

Paul makes this extraordinary statement: "Imitate me, as I imitate Christ" (1 Corinthians 11:1, MLB). Through transformed lives, God channels divine, renewing grace. God uses committed disciples rather than argumentative polemics to generate more disciples. Our heavenly Father rejoices when people are converted, not merely convinced.

Scripture, however, convinces, brings conviction, and effects conversion. Information establishes a foundation for conviction. Christianity is not some mindless religion associated with emotionalism divorced from reality. Other religions may bypass the brain, relying on meaningless experiences devoid of substance.

Authentic conversion paints a vastly different portrait. The genuine conversion experience is rational, rooted in actuality, defined by verifiable evidence. Paul writes, "I beseech you therefore, brethren, by the mercies of God, that ye present your bodies a living sacrifice, holy, acceptable unto God, *which is* your reasonable service" (Romans 12:1, KJV; emphasis added).

The word *service* derives from the Greek expression $\lambda \alpha \tau \rho \epsilon i \alpha \nu$, from which the modern, albeit obscure, theological term *latria* comes. *Latria* connotes adoration, reverence, an internally motivated worship as contrasted with external ceremonies associated with worship. Paul defines this worship using the adjective $\lambda o \gamma \iota \kappa \eta \nu$, from which the contemporary expression *logical* is derived. A worship-based lifestyle (genuine conversion) is, therefore, foundationally reasonable, rational, and rooted in reliable information. Although several modern translations render this passage "spiritual worship," which is plausible, the King James's focus on reason and rationality seems closer to the original intent and context. *The Revised English Bible* also seems sensitive about this rational-thinking emphasis, and translates it, "the worship offered by *mind* and heart. Conform no longer to the pattern of this present world, but be transformed by the renewal of your *minds*" (verses 1, 2; emphasis added). Similarly Isaiah quotes God addressing Israel: "Let us reason together" (Isaiah 1:18). The word translated as "reason" comes from the Hebrew *yakach,* terminology commonly utilized in legal disputes where lawyers argue from evidence, truth, and verifiable reality. While recognizing the importance of convincing, the disciple-maker will nevertheless understand that this falls short of the ultimate goal of converting.

In attracting disciples, Jesus understood the power of Scripture to convince. With this in mind, Jesus worked to establish His Messianic identity at the beginning of His ministry. Freeing fear-filled hostages is difficult whenever they fail to recognize their Rescuer. Therefore, this was a core objective. What methodology did Jesus employ to accomplish this important goal of convincing Israel? Being divine, Christ might simply have overwhelmed them with a glorious self-revelation. Likewise, Jesus might have depended entirely on incredible miracles that proved His identity. Or, being all-powerful, He could have opted to force belief.

Instead, Jesus appealed to the Bible. Scripture records,

> The book of the prophet Isaiah was given to him. And Jesus opened the book and found the place where it is written, "The Spirit of the Lord is upon me; because of this he has anointed me to preach good tidings to the poor; and he has sent me to heal the brokenhearted, and to proclaim release to the captives and sight to the blind; to strengthen with forgiveness those who are bruised and to preach the acceptable year of the Lord" (Luke 4:17–19, *Lamsa*).

Christ rolled up the scroll and, after returning it to the attendant, seated Himself. Presently everyone's gaze was centered on Jesus. Awkward silence settled over the synagogue. Then Jesus spoke, "Today this *scripture* is fulfilled in your ears" (verse 21, *Lamsa;* emphasis added).

Jesus' method of convincing was not primarily sensuous display, unbelievable showmanship, or personal charisma. The ultimate convincing was established through Scripture. This fact confused Christ's own disciples, who reasoned that Messianic power could merely be unleashed to *compel* devotion. When the Samaritan village failed to acknowledge Christ, the thundering disciples, James and John, inquired, "Lord, do You want us to command fire to come down from heaven and consume them?" (Luke 9:54, NASB). Jesus immediately repudiated such nonsense. Christ's method was appealing persuasively to people's thinking, not emotionally to people's apprehensions. Scripture, rather than intimidation, was God's instrument for changing people's minds.

One winter during the Festival of Dedication, Jesus' opponents accused Him of blasphemy. Rather than becoming defensive, Jesus appealed to Scripture. "Jesus replied, '*It is written* in your own *Scriptures* that God said to certain leaders of the people, "I say, you are gods!" And you know that the *Scriptures* cannot be altered' " (John 10:34, NLT; emphasis added; see also Psalm 82:6). Scriptural comprehension was Christ's primary weapon for effecting changed hearts.

Convincing and convicting are closely linked but not identical.

Chapter 1

Convincing connotes changed understanding; mental processes and decision making are paramount. *Conviction* goes further; heart and action become prominent.

James, Christ's brother, delineates this distinction.

> Someone will say, "You have faith and I have works." Show me your faith apart from your works, and I will show you my faith by my works. You believe that God is one; you do well. *Even the demons believe—and shudder!* Do you want to be shown, you foolish person, that faith apart from works is useless? . . . Faith was active along with his [Abraham's] works, and faith was completed by his works; and the Scripture was fulfilled that says, "Abraham believed God, and it was counted to him as righteousness" (James 2:18–20, 22, 23, ESV; emphasis added).

Contrast the convinced demons with the convicted patriarch Abraham. Who received salvation? Which was converted? Convicted people are first convinced people. They have reviewed the evidence, considered alternatives, and ascertained truth. Demons, however, also believe. The evidence is exceedingly convincing because it induces trembling; but these devils are *not* convicted. *Conviction* suggests an important step beyond mere recognition; it implies a compulsion to admit truth, a conscientious inclination toward accepting that truth, an invitation for heartfelt action. The playing field has switched from brain to heart, from mind to conscience. Both Abraham and the demons were convinced about the Messiah's identity. This provoked even fiercer opposition to Christ among the demons but humble acceptance of his Deliverer for Abraham.

The knowledgeable disciple-maker will recognize this important distinction between *convincing* and *convicting*. Plausible arguments, cogent reasoning, and incontrovertible evidence are powerful allies in the cause of convincing, but they are powerless to generate conviction. Many well-intentioned and would-be soul winners are baffled and frustrated whenever their clear presentations of truth fail to bring about conviction. While evidence may convince, only God's Divine Spirit brings about that twinge of conscience called conviction. Sometimes anxious relatives, understandably concerned regarding their family's spiritual welfare, deposit truckload upon Dumpster-load upon landfill-load of biblical information upon their increasingly alienated loved ones. Tracts, magazines, and brochures land unread in the garbage. Acquaintances confess that they understand biblical truths yet do nothing. Discouraged disciple-makers resign themselves to failure and often quit altogether. Because they depended on the rationality of their arguments, they are forced to concede defeat.

This is unnecessary. Intercessory prayer, through which we acknowledge our dependence upon God's Spirit to effect conviction, should become the springboard for *every* attempt at disciple-making. This accomplishes three things: First, it protects the soul winner against the temptation to glorify the human presentation of truth. Skillful presentations, divorced from divine power, are impotent. Second, it relieves the disciple-maker from the responsibility of making converts. Needless guilt and frustration frequently attend those who assume this responsibility themselves. Third, and most important, it releases heavenly power and influence on behalf of the persons we pray for. (Chapter 3 is devoted to intercessory prayer within the context of disciple-making.)

Are sloppy, poorly organized, unsubstantiated presentations of biblical truth therefore acceptable because God's Spirit alone can bring conviction? While gospel treasure is distributed through clay pots, fewer treasures get delivered wherever those pots have holes. Holes in reasoning, missing pieces of evidence, unenthusiastic delivery of truth, and so on, are completely unacceptable. We cannot expect God's favor whenever we excuse ourselves from reaching the highest standards. God's children have a sacred responsibility to deliver God's message with the best of their God-given abilities. Sometimes when attorneys inadequately represent their clients, judges declare mistrials. How many mistrials would be declared based upon our representation of Christ? Or to change metaphors, hunters cannot kill their prey without ammunition. Straight barrels are, nevertheless, critical to the enterprise. While God's Spirit alone can destroy sinful natures, Christians must allow Jesus to keep their barrels straight for the timely delivery of truth. Remember, Christ chooses to deliver life-changing, sin-destroying truth through you.

God proclaimed through Ezekiel,

"I have made you a watchman for the house of Israel. . . . If a righteous person turns from his righteousness and commits injustice, and I lay a stumbling block before him, he shall die. Because you have not warned him, he shall die for his sin, and his

14

righteous deeds that he has done shall not be remembered, but his blood I will require at *your* hand. But if *you* warn the righteous person not to sin, and he does not sin, he shall surely live, because he took warning, and *you* will have delivered *your* soul" (Ezekiel 3:17, 20, 21, ESV; emphasis added).

Every believer shares the watchman's responsibility. Our heavenly Father requires our best efforts.

I have coached track and field for a decade, winning three conference championships. Good coaches never expect their athletes to give them what they do not have, but they expect them to give everything they do have. Every season our athletes hear the same speech: "Your coaches will never criticize you for losing races; but they will never excuse you for giving less than your best." The disciple-making enterprise requires every God-given endowment for completing this divine assignment; nothing more, nothing less, nothing else.

Jesus understood the power of Scripture to bring conviction. An unnamed wealthy youth once questioned Christ regarding eternal life. Jesus responded, " 'Keep the commandments if you want to enter life.' 'What commandments?' he asked. Jesus answered, 'Do not commit murder; do not commit adultery; do not steal; do not accuse anyone falsely; respect your father and your mother; and love your neighbor as you love yourself' " (Matthew 19:17–19, TEV; see also Exodus 20:12–16; Deuteronomy 5:16–20; and Leviticus 19:18). The youth desired salvation, was obviously convinced of Jesus' Messianic identity or else he would have never asked the question, and was evidently convicted. We know that because Scripture records that Christ's appeal to him met a remorseful rejection. Remorse would have been absent had there been no conviction. Scripture, however, had accomplished its purpose. God's Spirit had employed the timeless commandments to awaken conscience and instill conviction.

Another prosperous individual requested a private meeting with Christ to inquire about eternal life. Characteristically, Jesus unlocked the Scriptures for His nocturnal guest. John recalls the conversation: "Just as Moses lifted up the snake in the desert, so the Son of Man must be lifted up, that everyone who believes in him may have eternal life" (John 3:14, 15, NIV; see also Numbers 21:7–9). Although years would pass before the scriptural seed planted that evening bore fruit, conviction had taken root, eventually leading to Nicodemus's conversion (John 7:50–52).

Conviction without action, however, cannot yield conversion. Conviction introduces the desire for conversion. That twinge of conscience urges us to accept Christ as our Deliverer. Nonetheless, until that decision is reached, the sinner is lost. The young aristocrat walked away from Christ remorseful but lost. King Agrippa was "almost persuaded" but lost (see Acts 26:28). Judas Iscariot was a "church member" but lost. As James suggests, action makes the difference. The action of accepting Jesus as one's personal Savior initiates the conversion experience. Conversion, like conviction, is God's divine work. Negotiating, cajoling, threatening, bribing, coercing through any means are useless to bring conversion.

Jesus' method was to present scriptural truth, however unpopular or politically incorrect it might have been. Righteous boldness characterized His presentation:

"You hypocrites!" Jesus said, "Isaiah was right when he prophesied about you: 'These people honor me with their lips, but their hearts are far from me. They worship me in vain; their teachings are but rules taught by man' " (Matthew 15:7–9, NIV).

For Christ, Scripture was the standard by which truth was determined. Truth brought conviction. Those accepting truth were converted, but that acceptance was seldom immediate:

Many of the leaders put their faith in Jesus, but they did not tell anyone about it. The Pharisees had already given orders for the people not to have anything to do with anyone who had faith in Jesus. And besides, the leaders liked praise from others, more than they liked praise from God (John 12:42, 43, CEV).

That picture changed, however, after Pentecost. Luke writes, "The word of God was continuing to spread. The group of followers in Jerusalem increased, and a great number of the Jewish priests believed and obeyed" (Acts 6:7, NCV).

Scripture forms the bedrock of the disciple-making process in two distinct but interrelated ways: First, Scripture must be actively transforming believers' lives, equipping them to be channels of divine grace. Unfortunately, this primary work is frequently overlooked or quickly bypassed by those anxious to teach techniques, methodologies, and procedures. This tacitly assumes that convincing is the ultimate objective. The unconverted life, however, cannot truly bring new followers to Christ. Such efforts are manipulative at worst and well intentioned but short-sighted at best. Because their foundation is not fully scriptural, their outcomes are inevitably disappointing. Spiritual transformation informed by Scripture is not an optional accessory but the essential center of disciple-making.

Only spiritually transformed disciples are prepared for the second part of the process: facilitating the steps of convincing, convicting, and converting. Dedicated disciple-makers will prayerfully request divine tact, wisdom, and understanding when they disseminate the everlasting gospel so that even the greatest intellects will be convinced, the hardest hearts will be convicted, and the emptiest souls will be filled. Start to finish, this is a heavenly undertaking, not accomplished by human resolve but through God's Spirit alone. What incredible benevolence that God has commissioned us to join Him in this most wonderful adventure.

CHAPTER 2

Suppose a youthful suitor greatly admired a beautiful woman. Furthermore, this admiration was clandestine. Without hesitation, the suitor conversed with friends regarding this venerated beauty. Yet fear prevented him from ever approaching the object of his affection. This prolonged detachment continued unabated until one evening when a brilliant epiphany awakened him from slumber. An elaborate strategy emerged. Eagerly, he made the necessary preparations. Sparing no expense, he secured a mountaintop chalet with a panoramic view of the surrounding mountains, which were especially picturesque around sunset. The chalet itself was graciously furnished in lavish Victorian style, with extravagant chandeliers, expensive woodwork, and impressive draperies. The dining area was exquisite, particularly charming by candlelight. He employed high-priced Italian chefs and purchased the finest cuisine. French servants were appointed to attend the couples' every desire. A Juilliard string quintet was engaged, and a luxurious limousine was chartered to transport the couple to the mountain hideaway.

Curiously, during this period of intense preparation, the suitor never considered introducing himself to the attractive young woman. Surely the impressive display he had masterminded would impress her. The softly cushioned limousine would caress her, and the sparkling candlelight would dazzle her. She would be flabbergasted by his overly generous presents. The sumptuous banquet would astonish her; the soothing string harmonies would stimulate her deepest passions. Suddenly, she would experience an irresistible attraction toward her impeccably dressed suitor, instantly falling in love. From an adjacent parlor, a minister would appear, joining them in holy wedlock, eternal bliss, now and forevermore. Proceeding from the chalet, the enraptured couple would board his luxury helicopter and be whisked away for a romantic honeymoon on a remote island paradise. Why would such a promising future require an introduction?

The day finally arrived. Everything was ready. The limousine driver promptly delivered the suitor to the aforementioned fair maiden's doorstep. He virtually floated from the vehicle through the gateway, riding his romantic imagination. Sunlight peeked through clouds, striking the front porch as she departed for work. Who was this tuxedo-clad weirdo positioned on her doorstep? With a flourish, he invited her into the waiting limousine.

Very impressive, right?

Wrong. She was horrified. This complete stranger materializes at her apartment and expects her to accompany him. Kidnapper? Stalker? Pervert? Frustrated, the puzzled suitor repeated the invitation. Immediately the terrified beauty fumbled through her purse, desperately trying to locate her phone or pepper spray. The nonplussed suitor panicked and demanded that she enter the limousine. Why was his generosity not appreciated? Her reaction mystified him. Fearfully, she complied with his demands. The chauffeur hastened toward the mountain hideaway.

Once inside the limousine, the maiden variously screamed, cried, and threatened. She had stumbled into her worst nightmare: kidnapped by a stranger, forced into unfamiliar surroundings, headed for an unknown destination. The youthful suitor could not understand her "irrational" behavior. He had provided an incredible romantic adventure at considerable personal expense, and this was not appreciated. What ingratitude! His supreme expression of love—rejected! Eventually, she calmed down, wearied by emotional exhaustion. The limousine finally arrived at the secret destination. She completely missed its loveliness and naturalness. Once inside she tearfully excused herself to the bathroom, claiming she needed to retouch her makeup. She locked herself inside, located the phone inside her purse, and called for help. Tracing her cellular signal, the authorities quickly located the chalet, stormed the entrance, and arrested the well-intentioned but horribly misguided suitor.

Discipleship

Today he remains the lonely sole occupant of an abandoned island prison.

Years passed and a wiser suitor began paying attention to the aforementioned fair maiden. Enamored by her beauty, he sought every opportunity to get acquainted. Jogging by her parking space, he smiled and waved every morning. Although she ignored him initially, his winsome manner softened her. Eventually, she found herself waving back, weakly at first, but with increasing enthusiasm. Once upon a supermarket trip, their carts "accidentally" bumped and the second suitor utilized the "chance" occurrence to introduce himself. The young woman reciprocated, sharing information about herself. Next, they crossed paths at a locally owned and operated smoothie shop. That serendipitous meeting foreshadowed their first official date. The more she learned, the more she liked. Both endorsed green energy, enjoyed bicycles, valued reading, cherished family, and championed similar political viewpoints. She discovered they even shared mutual religious convictions.

This second suitor owned a beautiful chalet in a nearby mountain range. He longed to share it with his beloved. There he employed a high-priced Italian chef who stocked the cupboards with the finest cuisine and freshest smoothie ingredients. His attendants kept the mountain hideaway in immaculate condition and polished the exquisite furniture daily. The silver never tarnished, and the glassware never spotted. Gorgeous sunsets painted the oversized deck, and sunrises were equally spectacular. The limousine was tuned monthly for optimal performance. Using one description, then another, he glowingly portrayed his favored castle for his girlfriend. Brushstroke after brushstroke lured her closer to the canvas. Finally, she inquired about visiting and possibly staying. He knew what that meant.

Finally, the day arrived. The limousine driver dropped the wiser suitor on the girlfriend's doorstep. Sunshine landed lazily on the front porch. She exited animatedly—grinning, singing—loaded with suitcases that the chauffeur dutifully loaded into the vehicle. Overjoyed at her beloved's arrival, she floated into the backseat, cuddling happily. They leisurely drove up the mountainside, stopping occasionally to revel at natural wonders. After arriving, she excused herself to the bathroom. She extracted the phone from her purse and turned it off to avoid unwanted disturbances, retouched her makeup, and returned to her boyfriend's company to share a sumptuous repast. Afterwards, by the fireplace light, he proposed, she accepted, and the minister entered from an adjoining parlor to unite them in everlasting wedded bliss. His luxurious helicopter ferried them to a privately owned uncharted island paradise off the Belizean coast, where they still live with seven homeschooled children.

What made the difference? Preparation. Both suitors offered accommodations beyond description, gourmet meals, luxurious automobiles, extravagant gifts, and similar amenities. The first, however, elicited fear; the second love. Although their offerings were identical, their methodology was worlds apart. The second recognized that his world, although beautiful beyond comparison, was unfamiliar and unknown, and the unknown engenders fear and trepidation. Thus, the second suitor took time to transform, brushstroke by brushstroke, the unfamiliar into the gloriously commonplace. By utilizing the familiar (himself), he formed a relationship with his beloved that encouraged her to venture into the unfamiliar. That venture led to commitment, and that commitment led to paradise.

Like the suitors in the parable, modern disciple-makers face similar challenges. Unfortunately, many demonstrate complete insensitivity to the diverse cultural backgrounds and life experiences of their audiences. Like the initial suitor, they believe these truths are self-evident, needing no introduction. "Everyone with any sense should acknowledge that, only dummies could miss out." They fail to prepare the ground, planting seed prematurely, and then curse the soil for failing to sprout. They present truth as it was presented hundreds of years ago, using forgotten language, unknown traditions, and naive assumptions. Then they wonder why failure follows failure and blame industrialization, post-modernism, ineffective parenting, the eschatological times, secularism, and other handy scapegoats.

But laziness is the problem. Work is necessary to translate the gospel into forms that are faithful to historic truth but that relate to modern thinking. Most are content to merely repeat past creeds whose expression fails to communicate the gospel essence. The effective disciple-maker *must* master (not merely tinker with) scriptural truth and be firmly rooted in contemporary culture. As Christ was both eternal and human, so the contemporary believer brings eternal truth together with human understanding. The Word is made flesh whenever, in fulfillment of Romans 8:4, a human life is transformed by the grace expressed throughout Scripture.

The principle of incarnation—not that humans become God but that

Discipleship

God through Scripture transforms humankind—is thus ongoing with every faithful succeeding generation. Jesus effected the spiritual preparation necessary for scriptural transformation by using illustrations, parables, and metaphors that transported His audiences from familiar surroundings to spiritual truth. Although challenging and never easy, the modern disciple-maker will never be satisfied until he or she is doing likewise.

> Jesus spoke all these things to the crowd in parables; he did not say anything to them without using a parable. So was fulfilled what was spoken through the prophet:
>
> "I will open my mouth in parables,
>   I will utter things hidden since the creation of the world"
>   (Matthew 13:34, 35, NIV).

Christ differentiated between His proclamation to the masses and His presentation to the disciples. With somewhat prepared soil, exemplified by the disciples, He could be direct. Outside that inner circle, illustration and explanation became standard seed-planting strategies.

Today's disciple-makers likewise make that distinction. Because maturing believers have presumably entered the Christian world, they have learned the dialect, jargon, and scriptural and theological terminology. The uninitiated unbeliever cannot relate to this language because they did not grow up speaking "scripturese." Analogies, illustrations, parables, stories, and metaphors bridge that chasm. These begin with the familiar but venture into uncharted waters. They utilize commonplace stories, objects, and experiences to introduce additional concepts. Because unbelievers trust the familiar experience they willingly embrace fresh ideas associated with that experience.

Scripture employs metaphorical language and forms to accomplish a broad spectrum of redemptive missions. Sometimes parables mask some truth that might otherwise be readily rejected until defense mechanisms have been evaded and truth has penetrated the heart. At other times, metaphors explain complex concepts through understandable experiences and language. Illustrations may create a sense of wonderment or entice reticent seekers to plunge ahead. The sincere disciple-maker will study Scripture diligently in order to appreciate the value and various uses of metaphor for advancing God's kingdom.

For instance, *metaphor is used to disguise intent until truth has penetrated the heart*. The classic example is Nathan's confrontation with David (2 Samuel 12:1–7). Unlike Elijah, who would later defiantly challenge Ahab, Nathan employed a more subtle approach. (Generations later, Christ would utilize similar strategies when dealing with the Pharisees [e.g., Matthew 21:28–32; 25:31–45; Luke 10:25–37; 14:16–24; 18:1–8; 20:9–19].) David had publicly embarrassed Jehovah, murdered an innocent soldier, committed adultery with the soldier's spouse, and attempted to cover everything up. Nathan recounted the story of a shepherd peasant who owned a single lamb. The peasant's prosperous neighbor possessed extensive real estate, numerous livestock, and immeasurable wealth. When the prosperous neighbor received a traveler, instead of securing dinner from his considerable flocks, he butchered the peasant's only animal. David jumped into the trap, enthusiastically condemning the wealthy owner. Only then did Nathan deliver the punch line: "You're the offender!" The prophet unveiled the parable's intent, openly divulging the king's wicked actions: fornication, manslaughter, and concealment. Because the parable had elicited David's self-condemnation, he could be angry only with himself.

Consider the following modern-day parable couched in dramatic dialogue. How is truth concealed until reaching the punch line?

SKEPTIC.   Ha! So you really think that you have been talking to an-
           other intelligent being all this time?
BELIEVER. As a matter of fact, I *do*.
SKEPTIC.   So you just talk, and magically your voice rises into the
           heavens to be beamed on to someone who anxiously awaits
           your call?
BELIEVER. Exactly.
SKEPTIC.   Well, your naïveté is touching, but, really, isn't it time to
           come down to reality?
BELIEVER. Well, how do you explain the fact that I hear a voice on the
           other end whenever I call?
SKEPTIC.   Every time?
BELIEVER. Well, often enough—and I leave a message at other times.
SKEPTIC.   Really? Well I'm sure that it's comforting to believe that
           there really is someone out there who hears you and cares

	about you and answers when you call—but it's all just wishful thinking.
BELIEVER.	Wishful thinking?
SKEPTIC.	I'm not saying that it's bad. Some of us have just never have outgrown our security blankets. So, if it makes you feel better and more assured I'll not object—to your fantasy!
BELIEVER.	This is no fantasy.
SKEPTIC.	Just a piece of imagination. . . . Tell me, have you ever seen, touched, or held—
BELIEVER.	Touched or held? No; but up there beyond what we can now see with our eyes is something that is real. I've read about this from those who actually saw and touched for themselves before losing sight of the ascent into the heavens.
SKEPTIC.	Fairy tales, fairy tales. Where's your proof? Apart from the claims of a few visionary dreamers whose ideas can't be trusted, you have nothing. Your confidence is built on false hope.
BELIEVER.	So how do you explain the book? Why would so many people have their names in the book if, as you say, such communication doesn't exist.
SKEPTIC.	Lies, lies, lies! Your invisible world defies reason. If I can't see it, touch it, hold it, and explain it, it isn't real. Every thinking person agrees on that. You've just been parking your head in the brainwash too long. I'd have to be a fool to believe in *satellite phones!*[1]

Metaphor is used to illustrate spiritual truth and persuade. Christ's nighttime encounter with Nicodemus exemplifies this purpose well (John 3:1–21). This Pharisee revealed ignorance about spiritual things. To counteract this problem, Jesus used wind to illustrate a spiritual concept. Wind is invisible but its effects are noticeable. God's Spirit is likewise invisible, but spiritual transformation is undeniable.

While Nicodemus's conversion was not immediately apparent, his eventual commitment to Christ may be traced to that evening visit and the powerful visual imagery that Christ employed to convey truth.

Consider the following modern parable, set in dramatic form, that imagines a conversation between the wind and a puppet.

Chapter 2

WIND.   Wake up, puppet head. You look like a pile of rags.

PUPPET.   I *am* a pile of rags, and I can't get up. The only way I stand
              up is if someone wears me on his or her hand. Otherwise
              I'm just what you see right now—a flop.

WIND.   So?

PUPPET.   Well, I really don't want that grubby brat's hand to wear me
              again. I feel violated. He's always dirty and germy—never
              washes his hands. I'm already so filthy inside that I can't
              stand it.

WIND.   Can't stand up either?

PUPPET.   It's horrible, and you don't have to rub it in. No, I can't
              stand it, *and* I can't stand. The only way I ever get up is
              when *he's* in control. Some choice: Whenever I get up and
              get noticed, it means he's in charge of my every move. It's
              nice hearing kids laugh, but deep inside I know I'm just
              getting dirty. Otherwise I live like this, a total flop.

WIND.   You don't have to.

PUPPET.   Oh, I used to think so. I used to think there was a way out.
              I saw another puppet, and he was free as a bird. He didn't
              need the help of a hand to stand up, and he moved through
              the air with the greatest of ease. He looked so happy and
              free.

WIND.   And?

PUPPET.   It was all an illusion. When I got closer I could see it. There
              was no grubby hand helping him stand, but he was all tied
              up. There were strings attached everywhere—mouth, hands,
              feet. I had such high hopes. I just crumbled back to the
              ground—shattered. There was no freedom after all.

WIND.   But there is!

PUPPET.   Lies!

WIND.   No, I mean it. My family business is setting puppets free to
              soar.

PUPPET,   Really? I can't even see you.
skeptically.

WIND.   A little faith, how about it? What do you expect from the
              wind?

PUPPET.   Make your pitch.

WIND.   A family member paid the price for all puppets to live . . .

	even while you were still flops. Now you can go anywhere you want.
PUPPET.	And how much does this cost?
WIND.	Oh, it costs a ton! More than you could ever afford . . .
PUPPET.	Figures!
WIND.	. . . but it's free to *you*. A grant from the family foundation took care of it.
PUPPET.	No! Really?
WIND.	Really. And all you have to do is let me live inside you, and I'll clean out all of Grubby's dirty germs. . . . Don't worry, we only use nonchlorine bleach, since it's gentler.
PUPPET.	Really? Oh, I'll try anything. Do it! . . . Now! . . . Oh . . . I don't believe it . . . I didn't mean that—I really do . . . I'm filling up . . . I'm soaring . . . I'm free!²

Metaphor is used to paint a spiritual picture. To a greater or lesser degree, every authentic metaphor accomplishes this goal. Christ might have declared, "My Father distributes spiritual truth to everyone. How you respond is your responsibility." Instead, He shared an agricultural narrative about a farmer planting his crops. Jesus might have stated, "My Father loves you immeasurably and unconditionally." Instead, He chronicled a father's anguish at losing his younger son and his ecstasy upon finding him. The Messiah could have lectured His listeners about racial intolerance. Instead, the Master Storyteller transported His listeners to the Jericho highway, where they watched a despised Samaritan embrace a helpless Israelite and restore his fortunes. Symbolic metaphors similarly enrich our reading experience in Scripture. Peter's vision in Acts 10 assumes symbolic imagery. John's Revelation overflows with unforgettable apocalyptic symbolism. Jesus' brother James writes, "He will pass away *like* a wildflower" (James 1:10, NIV; emphasis added) and "Take ships as an *example*" (James 3:4, NIV; emphasis added). Paul illustrates with courtroom terminology, athletic imagery, and the jargon of commerce. Effective disciple-makers likewise paint pictures to enable honest seekers to grasp spiritual truth. "A picture is worth a thousand words," even when the paintbrush is words.

Effective disciple-makers will follow these disciplines to become more adept in these areas: *First, become thoroughly familiar with Scripture.* Metaphors can greatly enhance spirituality, but a metaphor incorrectly used can distort truth. *Second, stimulate creative thinking by studying creative thinking.* Immerse yourself in Christ's parables, modern parables, and creative literature. Learn to think imaginatively. *Third, practice the art of Christian meditation.* Fill your mind with God's created wonders by enjoying nature. Intentionally draw lessons from commonplace occurrences. Mine everyday events for spiritual messages. *Fourth, comprehend contemporary culture and modern minds.* Communication is a two-way street. Believers must not only understand Scripture, they must also identify with the pleasures and disappointments of those they would reach. Sometimes Christians should stop talking and start listening so they might gain understanding. *Finally, pray incessantly.* God promises to supply our words. His promises cannot fail.

Our human limitations might prevent us from having the right story or illustration to reach another mind, but God is all knowing and all powerful. He will provide those words whenever humans trust Him completely.

---

1.   Gerhard Pfandl, "Lesson 13: Confidence in the Prophetic Gift," *Adult Sabbath School Bible Study Guide, Teacher's Edition* 455, no. 1 (January–March 2009): 157, 159.

2. General Conference Health Ministries Department, "Lesson 2: The Power of Choice," *Adult Sabbath School Bible Study Guide, Teacher's Edition* 460, no. 2 (April–June 2010): 25, 27.

CHAPTER 3

Exhausted and worried that someone might summon the police, I conceded defeat. Constantly ringing the doorbell had not worked. Incessantly beating the door, likewise, proved ineffective. Where was Dad? What was happening? What more could be done to awaken him? Already tired from traveling through the night, I reconsidered driving across town to my sister's house. Curling up like a puppy inside my pickup truck, I eventually fell asleep. Hours elapsed until sharp rapping noises against the driver's side window aroused me. *Dad!* Anxiety shaped his countenance. Distraught and exhausted by the previous week's events, my father had collapsed onto his mattress, completely oblivious to my shouting, banging, and ringing. He had been inside all along. Something, however, was definitely wrong.

This should have been an unforgettable weekend but for positive reasons. Living some distance from my high school, I infrequently attended reunions. This year, special arrangements had been made with my younger sister, who graduated from the same school, so that we might attend together. When she failed to arrive, I learned that those plans had abruptly changed because my mother had suddenly fallen ill. Not understanding the seriousness of her condition, I visited with former classmates, thus delaying my departure. Later that evening I started off for Pensacola, Florida, where both my sister and parents were living. Arriving early the following morning, I had tried, unsuccessfully, to awaken someone—anyone—at their house. Presently Dad's worry-filled expression answered my questions before they were asked: "Where's Mom? How's she doing?"

Mother had been hospitalized. Unfortunately, her intestinal blockage had been misdiagnosed. This life-threatening condition had been dismissed as a noncritical ailment treatable with conventional medications. Gangrene, however, was already poisoning her system. Her normally energetic disposition had been displaced by uncharacteristic lethargy. This was becoming an unforgettable weekend for the wrong reasons. Emergency surgery was scheduled. The surgeon's Sunday morning golf outing was interrupted when the hospital summoned him.

We crumbled to our knees. Prayer was not foreign to our experience. Nevertheless, there was a heightened sense of urgency: momentarily our mother and Dad's spouse could abandon this earthly life. Nothing prepares you for that event. We earnestly implored God for her restoration. Although the physician's skills were important, healing was God's alone. Surgery lasted longer than anticipated, creating additional concern and anxiety. We prayed continually. Life hung in the balance. Although weary, we persevered in prayer. Emotionally we experienced bereavement, becoming increasingly skeptical of the operation's success. Finally, the surgeon entered the waiting room. He cautioned us that Mother's chances for survival were no better than fifty-fifty. Later he admitted the situation was even worse: the gangrene was so pervasive that survival was not expected.

The following week was an emotional roller coaster. I contacted the office to request a vacation extension, and canceled that week's appointments. Everything else paled in significance. Trepidation attended every step. Mother's death seemed imminent. We lifted earnest supplications to heaven: "God, please! We're not ready to lose Mom." Gradually, her condition improved. Every advancement, however small, brought rejoicing. These glimmers of hope encouraged ongoing petition. Heartfelt thankfulness now attended those prayers. Additional improvements came, fueling our growing confidence that Mother would recover. Although obviously weak, Mother could finally speak. Hearing her voice further increased our courage. God's divine providence was evident through all that transpired. Months, even years, would pass before Mother had completely recovered, but God's answer to our intercession was unmistakable. Mother still enjoys relatively good health one-quarter of a century later!

Mother's eternal destiny was never an issue. Her deeply rooted devotion to God surfaced through her Christlike character. The certainty of her resurrection was beyond debate. Our emotional investment regarded this life *only*. We earnestly prayed because we selfishly desired her earthly companionship for another twenty-five or even forty years. Our grieving, insomnia, and diminished appetites were our sentimental responses to temporary loss, but those responses were valid and appropriate. No compassionate person would question or ridicule our reactions during that difficult period.

Today I question myself because my daily routine does *not* reveal a similar emotional investment regarding the potential eternal loss for hundreds of people that I encounter weekly. What is your condition? Are you passionately invested in the eternal salvation of your fellow employees, classmates, neighbors, colleagues, and associates? Are you constantly interceding, morning and evening, for them? Are unconverted relatives and spiritually destitute friends the substance of daily prayer? While a large percentage of those who have studied Scripture with me have committed their lives to Christ, there are several who have not. I examine myself through the questions asked above: "Why don't I lose sleep over the uncommitted? Have I become self-satisfied because 'ninety-nine' have accepted Christ? Why isn't Christ's compassion for the lost 'one' burning uncontrollably in my heart?"

John recorded Christ's quintessential intercessory prayer:

"I pray not only for them [the twelve disciples], but also for those who believe in me because of their message. I pray that they may all be one. Father! May they be in us, just as you are in me and I am in you. May they be one, so that the world will believe that you sent me" (John 17:20, 21, TEV).

Jesus prayed that lost souls might witness a unified church and, thus, believe in Christ. How often have we petitioned God for Christian unity and been humble enough to sacrifice our cherished preferences to accomplish that objective? Does concern for lost souls supersede our egotistical desire for recognition and control?

Consider your congregation. Is Christ's standard of unity reflected there? Is Christ's loving message effectively replicated, thereby drawing bewildered souls into the kingdom? Does intercession occupy a central or peripheral position within the church? Before answering these last questions, let's examine the characteristics of intercessory prayer.

The primary distinguishing feature of effective intercessory prayer is its outward focus. Altogether too much prayer is inwardly oriented. God's children reduce heaven to Santa's palace and shrink prayer to divine shopping! "Lord, won't You buy me a Mercedes-Benz?" Personal desires, material needs, and self-centered requests dominate center stage. Time spent praying for others' spiritual condition is minimized.

Intercessory prayer, however, focuses on others. It draws us away from self-centeredness. Spiritual values become paramount, while lesser things fade away. This prayer evidences a divine miracle. Human beings are naturally self-centered. Divine grace is required to unshackle sinners bound by self-aggrandizement, self-absorption, and self-importance. Whenever believers intercede for others through prayer, it demonstrates God's power to transform human hearts. Unless the disciple-makers' hearts are first converted into an outward focus, our natural selfishness will undercut every effort to reach others.

Effective intercessory prayer is persistent. Paul admonished the Thessalonians, "Pray constantly" (1 Thessalonians 5:17, *Jerusalem Bible*). Jesus illustrated this principle, saying:

> Suppose one of you goes to a friend in the middle of the night and says, "Let me borrow three loaves of bread. A friend of mine has dropped in, and I don't have a thing for him to eat." And suppose your friend answers, "Don't bother me! The door is bolted, and my children and I are in bed. I cannot get up to give you something."
>
> He may not get up and give you the bread, just because you are his friend. But he will get up and give you as much as you need, simply because you are not ashamed to *keep on asking.*
>
> So I tell you to ask and you will receive, search and you will find, knock and the door will be opened for you. Everyone who asks will receive, everyone who searches will find, and the door will be opened for everyone who knocks (Luke 11:5–10, CEV; emphasis added).

Persistence does *not* demonstrate a faith deficiency. Some might reason, "Why bother God repeatedly? Does God need reminders?" This suggests that persistent prayer purposes to correct some divine shortcoming, as though God were forgetful. The purpose, however, does not reside in God's need but, rather, in human frailty. Repetition appears redundant to an uninformed casual observer. *Repetition appears redundant. Repetition appears redundant. Repetition appears redundant.* Doubtless, "repetition appears redundant" might become the only phrase you can repeat from this book if you read it repeatedly. But that's the whole point.

Athletes understand this principle. Take pole-vaulting, for example. This field event is, perhaps, the most complex series of motions in sports. Each motion must flow naturally into the next. Athletes practice the individual motions repeatedly, perfecting each before stringing them together. Muscle memory enables athletes to accomplish the complex transitions between individual motions flawlessly at the intense speed necessary for propelling the athlete above the crossbar. Without repetition, the process would be awkward and ineffective. Thus, repetition appears purposeful and necessary to the active participant and not to the casual observer. Persistent prayer does not make God more aware, but it prepares the disciple-maker to be more effective in life, faith, and witness. Intercession flows naturally from the believer's heart when practiced persistently.

Effective intercessory prayer is corporate. Jesus declared, "If two of you agree here on earth concerning anything you ask, my Father in heaven will do it for you. For where two or three gather together as my followers, I am there among them" (Matthew 18:19, 20, NLT). Even common wisdom teaches the value of togetherness. Solomon wrote,

> Two are better than one,
>> because they have a good return for their labor:
> If either of them falls down,
>> one can help the other up.
> But pity anyone who falls
>> and has no one to help them up!
> Also, if two lie down together, they will keep warm.
>> But how can one keep warm alone?
> Though one may be overpowered,
>> two can defend themselves.
> A cord of three strands is not quickly broken (Ecclesiastes 4:9–12, NIV).

Chapter 3

The immediate context of Christ's statement in Matthew is the development of Christian disciples. Christ's intended teaching was *not,* "Whenever three believers agree they need exotic sports cars, heaven will supply them!" His words dealt with correcting believers, effecting reconciliation, and restoring relationships. These concepts—correcting, reconciling, and restoring—are likewise foundational for everyone's relationship with God. Somehow, believers' intercessions influence spiritual outcomes in these three matters.

Some extreme interpretations should be avoided. First, praying for unbelievers does *not* automatically guarantee their salvation. Though hundreds should petition God regarding specific individuals, He does not override their power of choice. The object of intercessory prayer must still accept Christ to receive salvation. Prayer cannot compel another's conscience nor force conversion. Second, the attitude that intercessory prayer is useless should, likewise, be avoided. Some reason, "God already realizes they're lost. Telling Him about them does not increase His awareness. Why bother? Christ already loves them and is doing everything possible on their behalf. Praying won't generate additional divine activity." Though Scripture does not provide a detailed explanation of how intercessory prayer influences conversion, it unequivocally advocates such prayer.

In addition to Matthew 18, Scripture says,

> You want what you cannot have, so you murder; you are envious, and cannot attain your ambition, so you quarrel and fight. *You do not get what you want, because you do not pray for it.* Or, if you do, your requests are not granted, because you pray for the wrong motives, in order to squander what you get on your pleasures (James 4:2, 3, REB; emphasis added).

Paul corresponds with Timothy, saying,

> I urge that *petitions, prayers, intercessions,* and thanksgivings be offered *for all* men; for sovereigns and all in high office, that we may lead a tranquil and quiet life in full observance of religion and high standards of morality. Such prayer is right, and approved by God our Saviour, whose will it is *that all men should find salvation* and come to know the truth (1 Timothy 2:1–4, NEB; emphasis added).

Apparently, God delivers lost loved ones specifically responding to our petitions. Prayer does make a difference. Perhaps that transformation takes place in the person praying. The disciple-maker possibly becomes more intentional about reaching a person because he or she is praying for that person. Maybe the disciple-maker becomes more sensitive to unmet needs in the unbeliever's life because he or she is focused on the person through prayer. We might conjecture and speculate endlessly because Scripture does not offer a detailed analysis regarding the mechanics of intercessory prayer. Numerous passages, however, undeniably encourage it.

Satellite telephones are clearly outside the average person's technical expertise. This is just one illustration of technological gadgets people frequently utilize without knowing how they work. We might include wireless laptop Internet access, global positioning systems, and more mundane objects such as digital cameras and microwave ovens. Although people are unacquainted with the inner workings of these modern wonders, they do not hesitate to use them. Cameras take photographs, microwaves warm leftovers, and telephones connect irritated consumers with customer service agents in Pakistan, who then access their account information through computer links with American banks in Tallahassee—and people never question how this happens. Because these things work they are taken for granted.

Who swallows cold leftovers because they cannot explain how microwaves heat food? Yet, ironically, believers abandon corporate intercessory prayer because they cannot explain every detail. Perhaps the time has come for disciple-makers to merely accept Heaven's invitation to prayer and simply try it!

Effective intercessory prayer incorporates confession. The psalmist's lyrics instruct with the following: .

> Come and hear, all God-fearing men, as I tell what He did for me. I called aloud to Him, glorification on my tongue. *Had I an evil thought in my mind, the LORD would not have listened.* But God did listen; He paid heed to my prayer. Blessed is God who has not turned away my prayer, or His faithful care from me (Psalm 66:16–20, Tanakh; emphasis added).

The New Testament concurs.

Anyone who is having troubles should pray. Anyone who is happy should sing praises. Anyone who is sick, he should call the church's elders. They should pray for and pour oil on the person in the name of the Lord. And the prayer that is said with faith will make the sick person well; the Lord will heal that person. And if that person has sinned, the sins will be forgiven. *Confess your sins to each other and pray for each other* so God can heal you. When a believing person prays, great things happen (James 5:13–16, NCV; emphasis added).

Human sinfulness constitutes a barrier erected between God and humanity, and between all people with each other.

During my childhood, my father built an electrical motor and taught me basic electrical principles. Insulation prevented electrical currents from reaching certain places, thus preempting short circuits. In much the same way, sinful indulgences create a spiritual "insulation" that prevents "heavenly currents" from reaching hearts. Acknowledging sin, sincerely repenting, and seeking forgiveness enables the disciple-maker to effectively remove hindrances against divine grace.

Daniel's humility is eloquently expressed through the simplicity of his confession in Daniel 9:2–19. That confession acknowledges Israel's transgressions, pursues divine forgiveness, and accepts responsibility for their difficulties. Nevertheless, Daniel also expresses confidence in God's righteousness and mercifulness. His appeal is based upon God's promises rather than Israel's innocence. Intercessory prayer, likewise, acknowledges the sinfulness of the person praying, the iniquities of those prayed for, and accepts responsibility for the consequences. Attempts at rationalization, efforts to minimize responsibility, and similar undertakings, fashion an insulation that resists the effects of prayer. Our appeal must never be based upon human righteousness or innocence but solely upon God's graciousness toward His erring children.

Assessing your personal prayer life or your church's may prove painful. That assessment is, nonetheless, the initial step toward correction and ultimate effectiveness.

Focus

Does your church intercede for specific individuals who ignorantly or actively revolt against God? Is prayer's subject matter leaking roofs or abandoned hearts? Is your congregation preoccupied internally, praying only about the infirmities and obstacles encountered by believers? Does prayer pessimistically contemplate the world's degeneracy or optimistically anticipate the conversion of nonbelievers? Generally speaking, does prayer concentrate on *our* eschatological deliverance or the nonbeliever's spiritual transformation?

Frequency

Does your family or congregation practice intercessory prayer regularly or sporadically? Does intercession come naturally or artificially? Does praying for others feel awkward or contrived? Whenever intercession is unpretentious, instinctive, and spontaneous it happens effortlessly. Persistent prayer cannot happen whenever Christians doubt its efficacy. Guilt and shame cannot foster continued intercession. Haranguing believers about their indolence regarding intercession might induce temporary reforms but not long-lasting change. Only a heart anxious for God's glory and compassionately concerned for lost souls will persistently intercede. Only persistent intercessions effect spiritual change!

Form

Are individual members praying independently but not corporately? Is Paul's admonition, "Bear one another's burdens" heeded (Galatians 6:2)? Are the divine promises for gathered believers understood and appropriated? Is spiritual togetherness missing from your church's equation? Do small groups within the church meet on a regular basis, pleading for someone's salvation?

Forgiveness

If we confess our sins, he is faithful and just to forgive us our sins and to cleanse us from all our unrighteousness. If we say that we have not sinned, we make him a liar and his word is not in us (1 John 1:9, 10, *Lamsa*).

"If you forgive others the wrongs they have done, your heavenly Father will also forgive you; but if you do not forgive others, then the wrongs you have done will not be forgiven by your Father" (Matthew 6:14, 15, NEB).

Chapter 3

Does self-justification, not to mention self-righteousness, interfere with our intercession? Are appearances more important than reality? Do spiritual facades become obstacles to genuine confession and authentic transformation? How preferable the humility of honest confession compared with the pretentiousness that will not seek forgiveness!

Does intercession work? Does it ever!

Clayton Jepson is a retired minister whose physical stamina, because of advanced age, does not allow him to do the things he once enjoyed. Those limitations, however, do not inhibit his prayer life. He organized a group of believers from his retirement community who pray regularly for a supplied list of people. Everyone with whom the pastor studies the Bible is listed. People who struggle to overcome various barriers to fellowship with God are listed. Nearly fifty people on that list have been baptized during the last three years, accounting for most of those whom the pastor has baptized.

Even closer to home is the testimony of the author's son. Like many pastor's children, he drifted away from a living relationship with Christ and became enamored with the world. Then a nearly fatal automobile accident occurred. During the ensuing months of recovery and rehabilitation, he had abundant time for reflection and self-assessment. God pursued him and brought him home, spiritually speaking. An integral component of that transformation was intercessory prayer—not only the ones expected from parents and siblings—but from people around the world who heard about his accident. His heart was touched because so many people were praying for him.

CHAPTER 4

One by one Paul had watched his children, their cousins, and other young relatives accept Jesus Christ as their Savior and unite with the church. Now the Holy Spirit was calling him to make a decision, and he was accepting the invitation. A few years before that life-changing day, Paul had begun sending his children and a few other relatives to a Christian summer camp program sponsored by a church near the city where he lived. Day by day, the children heard stories of faith that inspired them. They learned that God loved them and that He had a purpose and plan for their young lives. After the second summer of camp ended, three of the older boys in the family became involved in an in-depth Bible study with the summer camp director. Following months of study, the young men accepted Christ as their Savior and were baptized. The following summer several of the girls in the family and another boy expressed an interest in committing their lives to Christ. The summer camp director initiated a weekly Bible study with the entire extended family, which included the three boys who had been baptized the previous summer. After several months of careful study, seven of the other young people requested baptism.

Often during the studies Paul had slipped in, observed, and listened to the discussion. The camp director was not sure if Paul approved, disapproved, or just wanted a place to sit. Paul never, with either a comment or even with his body language, betrayed his feelings. He was present months later when the camp director completed the series and asked the young people how many of them still wanted to offer their lives to Christ.

Every one of the seven affirmed their prior commitment but, before the camp director could leave, Paul confronted him with these words: "Is it OK for me to be baptized too?"

Christians often talk about the importance of parents presenting a godly example for their children in order to influence them to accept Christ; but here was a case when the decisions made by young people influenced a parent to request baptism. The following summer Paul not only sent his children and relatives to the camp but reached out to a neighbor's child and sponsored her for camp. She also began studying with the camp director.

The influence of children in the disciple-making process is often undervalued. A children's ministry director who was trying to involve a pastor in a children's discipleship program was met with these words: "I really don't have the time. I believe that God has called me to spend more time doing evangelism!" The pastor's attitude suggests that God is interested in only making adults disciples.

Consider the logic behind such an attitude. It would seem that the pastor is saying, "Let's wait until we have some adult-size problems before we try to lead people to Christ. Let's wait until they've become scarred with unwanted, out-of-wedlock pregnancies; alcohol abuse; years of useless, profane living; and then let's tell them about the matchless grace of Jesus. Let's wait until they've wasted more than half their lives and developed hard-to-break habits before we reveal God's grace. Let's chase them when their souls are calloused against the gospel, and their lifestyle imprisons their feeble motivation towards good instead of approaching them when their hearts are tender and pliable, unfettered, and more inclined toward good!"

Who else follows such logic? Does the dam inspector wait until a crack is spurting water, or does he or she act whenever the smallest imperfection is detected? Is God honored better by the last thirty years of a person's life than He would be by a lifetime of eighty or ninety years well lived? Should believers not remember that whenever young people are effectively reached that they may be spared the spiritual scarring that often accompanies those years not committed to God?

Studies that cross denominational lines indicate that relatively few people commit their lives to Christ after they have passed their teen years. Actually, most commitments to Christ occur before the teenage years. Ironically, some parents—those to whom God has entrusted the spiritual guardianship of youth—adopt the attitude stated by these words: "Well, let's not force religion down their throats. When they're older, they'll choose for themselves."

These parents, however, display completely different attitudes concerning education, financial planning, and other important matters. Where are parents saying, "Let's not force education down their throats? When they're older, if they're interested in reading, learning mathematics, or balancing their checkbooks, they can pursue an education then." Contrarily, many parents engage their children in formal education before their fourth birthday. Should not spiritual interests receive similar emphasis? Is that education which prepares people for seventy years of living more important than that which prepares them for eternity? When studies by virtually every denomination indicate that the prime opportunity for spiritual decision-making lies somewhere between the ages of eight and thirteen, should not evangelistically minded Christians mobilize to exploit this opening?

When the disciples chastised parents who brought their children for Christ's blessing, Jesus' disciples were prototypical for many contemporary Christian executives. Today's more politically correct leadership might be less discourteous, but their apparent priorities align perfectly with Christ's earliest followers: "God's church has considerable dimensions that demand enormous amounts of time. Managing substantial properties, sizeable sociopolitical agendas, and significant theological discussions requires an immense investment. Producing elaborate visioning statements, crafting viable mission strategies, and monitoring massive organizational networks necessitate extensive resourcing. After reviewing important, though cumbersome financial statements, evaluating voluminous demographic information, and assessing contemporary religious and cultural currents, who has time for kids?" Contrast Jesus' personal attitude: "Let the little children come" (Luke 18:16, NRSV). Christ's priorities differed sharply compared with His disciples. Children came first.

When our first grandchild entered the world, we were suddenly thrust into the technological world of neonatology. Neonatal intensive care units are unique blends of humanity's noblest efforts to preserve and sustain life coupled with the emotional desperation experienced by anxious parents. Grandson Noah was engulfed in wires, patches, tubes, and monitors—advanced technology serving the purpose of life through extreme circumstances. Other children admitted there could have been contained within a single hand. Their lives hang in unseen balances, and emotional equilibrium shifts moment by moment.

What precipitates this extensive concern for preserving physical life? Why have researchers refused to surrender these children to certain mortality, instead pushing the boundaries of technological intervention still further? What motivates this enormous investment of resources? Why have physicians not advised mothers to "accept the inevitable rather than fighting fate," instead developing ever more ingenious methodologies for sustaining life? While the medical community has vigorously pursued the knowledge that preserves young physical lives, why has the religious community not been equally aggressive in pursuing newer methods for preserving spiritual vigor among youth? Perhaps seminaries should prioritize the development of "spiritual neonatologists."

How should God's church respond to the challenge of fostering and preserving spiritual life among the young? Many well-intentioned leaders and parishioners have employed an approach that has alienated rather than befriended youth for Christ. Typically this is some variation of behaviorism that focuses on obligations, regulations, and outward conformance to societal mores. Frequently, these are rooted in narrow-minded viewpoints. Somewhere in the distant "long ago" an elderly church leader urged his young Christian employee to forsake guitar playing because guitars were "the devil's instruments"! Play guitar, forsake everlasting life!

Nothing was mentioned regarding the nature of the music played. No explanation was offered to justify the blanket condemnation of guitars. Fortunately, the young man was dissuaded from neither his church nor his guitar. His instrument, instead, became a treasured means of expressing faith. Unfortunately, many young people have been driven away by such unsubstantiated black-and-white statements founded upon irrational fears and self-righteous judgments.

Whether the particular issue is percussion instruments, fashion modesty, leisure activities, or public worship, youth *must* be approached with Christlike kindness and nonjudgmental graciousness. Unilateral pronouncements should be replaced by reasoned dialogue. Ethical decisions and practical theology should be mutually explored, not unilaterally dictated. Older generations should have much to offer but little to push. Younger generations respond negatively to coercion but are susceptible to gentle persuasion. The ancient aphorism repeatedly proves correct: "Men convinced against their will, are of the same opinion still."

Churches that demonstrate Christ's love for youth will be characterized by several emphases. First, these *churches provide safe environments* for nurturing faith. Unfortunately, sexual predators target faith communities. Lawsuits and allegations across denominational boundaries underscore the pervasiveness of such activity. Christ declared,

> "Occasions for stumbling are bound to come, but woe to anyone by whom they come! It would be better for you if a millstone were hung around your neck and you were thrown into the sea than for you to cause one of these little ones to stumble. Be on your guard! If another disciple sins, you must rebuke the offender" (Luke 17:1–3, NRSV).

Zero tolerance of inappropriate sexual activity *must* become every church's standard. Forgiving past indiscretions should never be confused with allowing such people access to youth groups, children's ministries, youth choirs, or scouting-type groups. The lasting psychological damage inflicted through premature sexual encounters has permanently scarred many young people. These emotional catastrophes interfere with future marital happiness, normal psychosocial development, and ordinary relationship formation.

Ensuring safe environments requires considerable diligence. Everyone who participates in any youth-related ministry should be vigorously screened by using services that provide thorough background checks. Just because someone finished medical school, graduate school, or even seminary does not necessarily certify that person's credibility. Anyone objecting to such measures should be denied access to youth. Some might question the necessity of such screening. Some volunteers might resign their positions, thus crippling already understaffed ministries. Most volunteers, however, will heartily endorse such procedures because they have heavily invested themselves in ministries that they do not want to see compromised by predatory activity.

Providing safe environs, however, implies much more than merely eliminating sexual predators. Safety also encompasses a broader attitude that encourages feelings of emotional comfort where youth can ask difficult questions, discuss domestic struggles, express negative feelings, and experience that awkward transition to adulthood without fear of condemnation. Providing safety might also include protecting youth from overzealous church members whose sole life mission is projecting their own insecurities and vulnerabilities onto the youth under the guise of counsel and guidance. Whenever belittling, condescension, and manipulation are involved, be assured that nobody is being "guided." Vocal attacks, anger, and derogatory remarks may also be telltale signals that intervention is required.

When seedlings are exposed to harsh weather conditions, poisons, heavy foot traffic, or other environmental hazards, they often meet their demise. Should that seedling reach adulthood that mature tree might withstand tornadoes, hurricanes, tree-house manufacture, tree swings, and aggressive trimming. Children are no different. The critical years are those early ones. Create a positive, nurturing environment that carries children successfully to adulthood and they will withstand negative criticism, personal suffering, and financial setbacks. Cripple children in their youth and they will be hampered for a lifetime.

Churches that love youth generally support another emphasis: *incorporating youth into the church's mission*. These churches are *not* saying that youth are the church of the future. They recognize that youth are the church *today*. Secular marketing recognizes the effectiveness of peer influence. Analyze advertisements for teenage clothing. Does marketing target teenagers or their parents? Are clothing producers trying to influence parents to choose their products for their children? Or are they trying to influence teenagers to influence their friends to purchase their products? Most would recognize the second strategy as the correct answer. Teenagers more often influence their parents' wardrobe choices than the reverse. They effectively create a counterculture that their parents finance.

Marketers exploit these phenomena, utilizing youth to persuade youth who persuade (badger?) parents. Effective marketers actually initiate this process much earlier than the teenage years. They intentionally generate youth media programming, cultivate young singing/dancing "stars," and establish youth networking opportunities. Paul stresses in the final verses of 1 Corinthians 9 that athletes train for temporal prizes, but believers train for eternal rewards. This same reasoning is applicable here. Marketers spend millions achieving temporal objectives (increased sales), whereas Christians expend their energies for eternal purposes.

Or, at least, we should. However, few churches of any persuasion take youth movements seriously. Some religious parachurch organizations have adapted and are successfully exploiting this opportunity. For example, the National Bible Bee annually awards more than a quarter million dollars to children for memorizing Scripture. *Thrilling* understates the euphoria this writer experienced by spending an extended weekend hearing children and youth quoting nothing but Scripture at the national competition. Many of the participants learned about the program from other excited children who encouraged them to participate. Their example could be replicated through local church ministries; that is, if churches focused undivided attention on harnessing these talents and energies.

Such churches understand that youth are not the "future church" but unlit evangelistic dynamite. Youth revolutionize their peers' world and older generations too. Young people often reach calloused, skeptical individuals who would never be reached through traditional evangelism. Because most people who commit their lives to Christ make that decision before the teenage years, and because contemporary youth culture constitutes the single most pervasive influence on youth, should the church not focus the most creative talent, most extensive resources, and most generous support on developing an effectively trained spiritual armed forces?

Athletic trainers recognize that youth enjoy a window of opportunity that never returns. Military commanders mobilize and train pilots, special forces, and elite tactical groups before those enlistees reach the age of twenty-five. When will churches understand the value of doing likewise? When will churches awaken to the opportunities now sleeping inside its cribs?

Churches that effectively nurture young disciples *provide multiple opportunities for spiritual decision-making.* Mounting evidence suggests that more young Christians formulate their initial acceptance of Christ in retreat or camp settings than in other places. This does not undervalue the importance of other ministries such as weekly worship services, small groups, weekly Bible study groups, recreational activities, and music ministries. Elements of these ministries are often incorporated into retreats or similar special events. Nevertheless, facts substantiate the assertion that retreats and camps are the most effective instrument for initiating faith among young adherents. Why?

Perhaps the most obvious reason is *opportunity.* Overt calls for accepting Christ are commonplace at Christian summer camps. How often is that invitation extended at weekly worship services? How often are spiritual appeals presented at recreational activities? Unless the question is asked, how can we expect a response?

Another factor may be *reduced distractions.* Eliminating distractions would be ideal but is unrealistic. In retreat settings, away from uncontrolled television, portable gaming devices, miniature music players, and hundreds of other diversions, the human soul finally breathes freely. Reflection replaces entertainment. Focused thought displaces interruptions. Spirituality supplants amusement. Prayer revives when not competing with sports trivia, homework deadlines, social anxieties, and an endless list of disruptions.

A complementary factor is *increased exposure to divine realities*. Nature has oftentimes been called God's second book. Summer camps and retreats offer multiple exposures to divine majesty. Heavenly bodies obscured by intense urban lighting are revealed. The intricacies of vegetation, frequently overlooked or absent in metropolitan settings, point to a Divine Designer and Sustainer. Wildlife likewise directs attention to our Creator. Replacing the artificial settings associated with contemporary culture with God's created world cannot help but refresh spiritual vitality.

The fourth component would be *positive examples*. One person decides to follow Christ. That individual's decision influences another's. This snowballing effect, which often employs negative peer pressure against spiritual interests, becomes reversed and influences positive decisions. At Pentecost, someone was the first of three thousand. Somebody might suggest that those who followed were lemmings, mindlessly pursuing the earliest adherent. Actually, everyone was following the Holy Spirit's invitation. Additionally, 2,999 of them were influenced by another person's decision. That human influence does not invalidate the Spirit's summons. Christ employs human example and testimony to inspire people for discipleship.

These elements—providing abundant opportunities or invitations for discipleship, reducing distractions, increasing exposure to heavenly things, and utilizing positive influence and example—should provide the framework for every youth or young adult outreach. Christ Himself employed this approach by issuing multiple calls for discipleship (e.g., Mark 1:14, 17, 37–38), temporarily separating His disciples from distracting environments (Mark 6:30–32), drawing spiritual lessons from nature (Matthew 6:26–30), and using human influence advantageously for cultivating additional disciples (John 1:40–52; 4:39–42).

Likely there are creative means for replicating these experiences without pitching tents or renting cabins. Nonetheless, churches should recognize that currently retreats and summer camps form natural allies in supplying an atmosphere where these occur spontaneously.

Churches that intentionally provide safety, support, and spiritual opportunities for community youth (not merely church-family youngsters) have bright spiritual futures. Their growth is predictable and their internal dynamics are exciting. Conversely, churches that neglect these opportunities are dying. Which kind of church do you want yours to be?

CHAPTER 5

Futility and hopelessness had characterized his entire existence. Other children had frolicked and played while he longingly gazed outside his bedroom window. Growing older, he watched helplessly as neighboring teenagers successfully transitioned to adulthood, accepting apprenticeships in their chosen trades. Those dreams and pursuits attended whole-bodied people, not crippled, disfigured people such as himself. Wedding sounds periodically filled the neighborhood, reminding him about his undesirability. What woman would consider uniting with such a helpless, unemployable reject? Supporting children and a spouse was absolutely impossible. Normalcy by any definition was a shattered dream at best—a nagging nightmare at worst. Had God intentionally selected him to suffer excruciating torment (physically, socially, and mentally) for punishment?

Doubtless the descendants of Job's "friends" had insinuated that his sinfulness had effected these regrettable circumstances. Pitying, but probably embarrassed relatives sustained his physical needs, providing food, clothing, and other basic necessities. Soul nourishment, however, was different. What conversation could he supply that might interest normal people who worked, raised families, resented taxation, attended weddings, planted gardens, and attended the synagogue weekly? Life revolved around the limited routine of dragging himself about the house, eating enough to escape dying, and spiritually hemorrhaging amid his meaningless existence.

Chapter 5

Misguided mythologies likewise betrayed him. Many believed that angels periodically disturbed the bathwaters at Bethesda. The legend postulated that whenever this occurred, the first person who entered the waters would be healed. Destitute individuals without better prospects flocked to such places, desperately seeking miraculous healing. Having consulted physicians, utilized traditional medications, and exhausted their available financial resources, they mindlessly embraced these implausible remedies. Family, perhaps even friends, had transported him alongside the reputed shrine. Having deposited him there, they apparently abandoned him there too. Perhaps they waited several days, but eventually personal responsibilities beckoned and they left.

Presently nobody attended him and his prospects for touching the water first had completely disappeared. Probably hungry, and definitely isolated, he anxiously clung to superstition. Thirty-eight years of unrequited yearning would end shortly, dramatically, and instantaneously—but through totally unexpected circumstances.

Enter Jesus the Messiah. "Would you like to get well?" Christ queried. Obviously! Nevertheless, there were predictable obstacles. Completely crippled people were incapable of outracing people with lesser impediments into the water. This greatly diminished his chances for restoration. Perhaps he wondered why Jesus even questioned him. Was His motivation curiosity or genuine concern? Would Jesus possibly assist his efforts to reach the water first? Before he could speculate further, Jesus commanded him, "Stand up!" Immediately sensations never before experienced surged throughout his body. Strengthened muscles, invigorated nervous tissue, and a rejuvenated skeletal system propelled him upward, responding to the Creator's directive. Gathering his bedroll he leaped skyward, shouting praises. Christ quietly disappeared into the gathering multitude, who witnessed this astounding sight.

Subsequently Jesus encountered this man within the temple precincts. Note Christ's curious statement: "Stop sinning or something even worse may happen." What an interesting warning. What possible connection could exist between physical incapacity (disease) and spiritual integration? How did Jesus bridge from physical restoration to spiritual wholeness? What connection exists between physical wellness and Christian discipleship? Stated otherwise, How does Jesus' healing ministry produce dedicated disciples?

First, disease produces insecurity and dependence. Remember

Daniel's Nebuchadnezzar? Arrogant, boastful, self-sufficient, he credited himself with creating the incomparable Babylonian Empire. He personally attributed its magnificent splendors to his creativity and ingenuity. Was God acknowledged? Was Divine Providence recognized? Prideful Nebuchadnezzar acknowledged only himself. Then circumstances changed. Clinical lycanthropy, or something similar, struck Nebuchadnezzar. For seven years, the insolent monarch prowled around like a wild animal. Lacking humanness, a royal embarrassment, the disgraced potentate had become thoroughly humiliated. He had fallen from favored sovereign to laughingstock. Even peasants and servants bore more respectability than he did. This tragic situation was unnecessary until Nebuchadnezzar's overflowing egotism allowed God little choice but either to relinquish him eternally or humiliate him in a way that would redeem his soul.

Our compassionate Savior, unwilling that any should perish, chose suffering that Nebuchadnezzar might repent and receive salvation. Afterwards the humbled monarch was restored. Rather than ignoring God, the king exalted and praised God for the rest of his life. Henceforth he acknowledged his dependence upon God's merciful favor and graciously recognized God's dominion and authority. Disease stripped Nebuchadnezzar's self-dependence and self-importance and offered an opportunity for redemption. Doubtless, Nebuchadnezzar's happiest years were those that followed his disease, healing, and spiritual reorientation.

Unfortunately, disease does not always bring similar results. A curious instance of disease having the opposite effect comes during Asa's kingship. The narrative contained in 1 Kings 15:9–24 praises his reign unequivocally. The parallel narrative in 2 Chronicles 14–16, however, supplies an interesting additional detail. During the closing stages of his administration, Asa contracted a severe foot disease but failed to seek divine intervention, trusting the physicians exclusively. Tragically, the once humble God-fearing sovereign stumbled and had this negative commentary added to his record near the conclusion of his reign. Disease and adversity essentially reveal the person's authentic character. Nebuchadnezzar's response was genuine conversion and God-dependence, while Asa's response revealed character defects of self-dependence and spiritual poverty.

Second, disease often exposes violations of natural law. Lung cancer victims are most frequently victims of their willful indulgence of smoking tobacco, though, of course, some who have never smoked a day in their lives still get the disease. Venereal diseases, some avoidable accidents, some types of obesity, and numerous other conditions can reveal spiritual and moral transgressions. Sometimes these transgressions were committed ignorantly. My father, now in his nineties, smoked cigarettes years before the surgeon general declared their cancer-producing properties. Nevertheless, smoking was damaging his health until he finally quit.

Unfortunately, those who suffer are not necessarily limited to the transgressors. When Satan issues billing statements for transgressions, he includes the transgressors' families, communities, and countries. Smokers cripple their children with secondhand smoke. Violent tempers can create ulcers inside the angry person and disseminate emotional indigestion among spouses, children, and other family members. Sometimes multiple generations make payments for sins committed by individuals. Disease, whether social, mental, physical, emotional, or otherwise, indicates sin's presence. We cannot corroborate Job's "friends" assertion that individual sinfulness necessarily causes every malady, but this does not disallow the principle that transgression causes disease. The transgression may be someone else's.

These principle characteristics of disease—that illness fosters divine dependence and sinfulness causes sickness—inform our understanding of Christ's healing ministry. Understanding them protects against fanatical fascination with spectacular healings and guards against dismissing divine intervention altogether. Jointly they shape Christianity's approach to healing, medicine, and restoration. Christ's understanding of human personhood was holistic. Our physical aspects were intertwined with, rather than separate from, our spiritual and emotional aspects. The Greco-Roman dualistic interpretation of personhood, radically dividing soul from body, was foreign to Christ's thinking and teaching. This interpretation regarded the "spiritual soul" as separate from the "degenerate body."

Logically this perception steered toward two different, but equally damaging, conclusions. First, the degenerate, wicked body must necessarily be disciplined, severely punished, or chastised in order that the spiritual nature would not be impeded or sullied. This might be accomplished by fleeing immoral society (monasticism) or personal punishment through physical self-flagellation, inflicting self-guilt, or psychological self-torture. Another conclusion suggested that because the body was inconsequential compared with the spiritual nature and effectively separate, it could participate in unspeakable forms of debauchery without affecting the essential spiritual being. Religious confession through earthly priesthoods frequently became the outlet "valve" to relieve the psychological pressure that accumulated through such egregious living. Christ's teaching advanced a completely different construction. Human personality in varying dimensions—physical, emotional, spiritual, mental, social—was interrelated, meaning each dimension would profoundly affect the others. Thus, in Christ's thinking, physical healing was never essentially divided from spiritual restoration.

The Greek word most often translated as "save" in Scripture, σῴζω (pronounced *sōzō*) embodies numerous concepts not commonly identified with the notion of "being saved." Generally speaking, these concepts are nonreligious; included ideas would be preservation and rescue from natural dangers, deliverance, releasing from disease, and, when passively conjugated, thriving, prospering, attaining wellness. Obviously, religiously speaking, spiritual salvation is included. Because *sōzō* represents both spiritual and physical restoration, the linkage between these aspects of human nature should become apparent. Physical deliverance and cleansing accompanies spiritual deliverance and cleansing. Jesus' statement to those He healed, "Go and sin no more," reveals the connection between spiritual disease and physical infirmity. Medical histories document multiple instances of physical diseases caused by spiritual dysfunction. Hatred, guilt, shame, and anxiety have contributed to emotional disorders, sleeplessness, obesity, and suicide. Dualism contradicts reality by challenging the obvious: our natures are intertwined and efforts to disregard this fundamental fact unnecessarily obstruct the complete restoration God provides.

By affecting the complete spiritual restoration of health and serenity, Jesus came to remove the wretchedness of disease and the burden of immorality. Humanity's drunken flirtation with lawlessness required the ultimate punishment. Just as blood transfusions preserve physical life, so the life transfusion through Christ's blood provides eternal salvation. Blood banks, however, are worthless unless there are blood recipients. Christ's sacrifice would appear pointless without life recipients. Therefore Christ became the heavenly Salesman, illustrating the divinely provided salvation through the means of physical healing.

Chapter 5

People in Jesus' day understood physical maladies. They watched friends perish. Extended illnesses, unexpected tragedies, warfare, natural disasters, and human violence engulfed the first century no less than they do the twenty-first. Through physical sickness, they sensed their neediness, helplessness, and hopelessness. Death's threatening shadow demanded their attention. Through partial restorations, illustrated by physical healing, Jesus the Messiah pointed toward the complete restoration made possible through divine forgiveness and supernatural power for overcoming sin's temptations.

Miraculous healing was *never* the ultimate objective. Such wonders were stepping-stones that guided spiritual travelers from recognized physical deficits to bodily wholeness, to recognizing spiritual imperfections, to comprehending the complete spiritual transformation and healing available from Heaven's storehouse. Unfortunately, popular healers regularly depreciate this divine endowment, substituting showmanship and entertainment for authentic revival and repentance. Such programs direct attention toward the so-called healer, effectively diverting attention away from the healing God, who requires surrender, repentance, and reformation.

Christ's example should educate sincere believers. If the Messiah was unsatisfied with attracting attention to Himself as a mere wonder-working healer, why should modern believers become enamored with self-proclaimed healers? Should spectacular healings secure human allegiance when such events are missing the greater objectives of repentance and authentic spiritual conversion? When such healings become ends in themselves, their value immediately diminishes.

Remember, however, that so-called faith healers are not alone in missing Christ's comprehensive view of healing. The secularization of medical practice was primarily caused by physicians who would quickly distance themselves from roadshow medical quackery but who, ironically, shared its spiritual blindness. Although disguised differently—*Marcus Welby, M.D.* replaced *Elmer Gantry;* stone-cropped buildings uprooted canvas evangelistic pavilions—the error was nearly identical. So-called faith healers made their crusades ends in themselves. Their objective was physical healing, nothing more (except, perhaps, collections from unsuspecting faithful attendees). Modern medicine has largely supplanted these self-credentialed "doctors" but has established physical health as the limited objective. Once bones are mended or cancer arrested, the objective has been reached. The broader canvas involving total restoration is ignored. Spirituality is forgotten.

How terribly ironic. For generations, medical progress and the establishment of hospitals was spearheaded by mission societies, parachurch organizations, charitable religious institutions, and the church itself. Hospitals, clinics, and sanitariums hardly existed without them. Their mission was clearly not limited to mending broken bones and reducing raging fevers. Following Jesus' example, they existed to employ physical healing as the means whereby complete restoration could be affected. Their essential purpose was spiritual. Subsequently, the means became the objective instead. The broader picture was submerged underneath a fascination with medical technology, anxieties regarding medical compensation, and the emerging consensus that medicine was scientific rather than spiritual. The founding organizations succumbed to this emerging consensus with hardly more than scattered whimpers. Churches abandoned medicine to civil government and civic organizations.

Nevertheless, modern Christianity may yet emulate the original model rather than the secularist's substitution. Certain concepts characterize the approaches of contemporary believers who recognize the incredible potential of health ministry.

1. They acknowledge the bigger picture of healing ministry, whose ultimate objective reaches well beyond physical restoration to spiritual transformation. Smoking cessation, mending broken limbs, encouraging physical exercise, and fighting cancerous tumors are important puzzle pieces within the divine scheme, but independently they are insufficient expressions of the broader purpose. Today's medical evangelist understands that greater spiritual truths must be shared. Eradicating cancerous tumors might extend longevity for fifteen more years. What then? Death postponed does not equal death eliminated. Christians have much to offer beyond temporary medical fixes. Should a starving, homeless indigent receive fifteen dollars from a passing stranger he might be very excited until he watched him disappear in a limousine. Then our disgruntled indigent might complain about receiving so little from someone with incredible wealth. When believers conceal the spiritual dimensions of healing because they fear personal or professional rejection, they withhold the spiritual treasury that Divine Providence has entrusted to their care. How might our friends or clients reevaluate our generosity should they discover that we withheld the most important aspects of healing?

2. They recognize that sin causes sickness. Germs, accidents, genetic inheritance, and other things are definitely contributing factors. Nevertheless, our sinfulness must be considered the ultimate culprit. Genuine healing is incomplete without an invitation to repentance. Thoroughgoing health is not achieved apart from spiritual cleansing. Sometimes the responsibility of forthright disclosure places the believer in the awkward position of correcting others. When this becomes necessary, the gentleness and humility described in Galatians 6:1, 2 is critical.

3. Christians involved in healing ministries are time sensitive. They understand that illness opens windows of opportunity that will not always remain open. During seasons of spiritual dependence, the believer *must* act promptly and judiciously to advance spiritual truth while favorable circumstances exist. Evil forces are working continuously to close those windows. Farmers carefully follow weather advisories, evaluate soil conditions, and maintain their machinery because timely planting is critical for bountiful harvests. Single seeds, properly nurtured, produce generous results. Following the restoration of Peter's mother-in-law in Matthew 8, "*many* demon-possessed people were brought to Jesus" (verse 16, NLT; emphasis added). In the twenty-eighth chapter of Acts, Luke writes, "Publius's father was ill with fever and dysentery. Paul went in and prayed for him, and laying his hands on him, he healed him. Then all the other sick people on the island came and were healed" (verses 8, 9, NLT).

Our family has witnessed the transformational healing power of God restoring physical and spiritual life. At the conclusion of chapter 3, there was a brief sketch about an accident my son suffered. The evening of that accident, our family had planned a dinner celebration honoring our younger son's birthday. That afternoon we received the phone message every parent loathes. While returning from his workplace, our older son had encountered gale force winds, and he lost control of his vehicle. He was ejected onto the highway after it flipped three times. The responding paramedics believed he would not survive. Some personal friends happened upon the accident and forewarned us. Once the ambulance arrived, the emergency physicians informed us that extensive trauma required transportation to another hospital where advanced care was available. We were not allowed on the helicopter. The ensuing drive was easily the longest trip of our lives.

Would he be alive when we arrived? Asphalt was deeply embedded within his skull, nearly every rib had been fractured, half his face resembled raw hamburger, and X-rays revealed spinal column damage. Our apprehensions were heightened because of his spiritual condition. Would death remove him *forever*? Contemplating your children's demise is extremely difficult when possessing eternal hope, but virtually unbearable whenever their spiritual condition is doubtful. Miraculously, he survived. Painful weeks of rehabilitation followed. Three hospitals and hundreds of thousands of dollars later, he was finally discharged. After six months, his rehabilitation physicians permitted limited part-time employment.

Like Nebuchadnezzar, our son had become absolutely dependent. For weeks, someone else fed him. For several months, someone else transported him. Others maintained his payments because of his unemployment. His schedule also allowed extended time for personal reflection. Questions demanded answers. What might have happened had he perished? Which eternal destiny awaited him? The prayers of acquaintances and strangers alike deeply impressed him. The Divine Comforter was softening his heart, bringing forth renewal just as the Divine Healer was actively, albeit gradually, restoring his physical being. Fractures mended, cranial pressure reached normalcy, asphalt was extracted, and the spinal column healed. More importantly, the lost son returned home to his heavenly Father's embrace. Today, this former wanderer would gladly tell you how grateful he is for the accident that almost killed him.

Perhaps other wandering children should also experience that embrace. Are you, perhaps, God's twenty-first-century Ananias, called to restore the health and spiritual eyesight of another wandering child? Ananias was God's chosen human instrument to restore the blind apostle Paul. What gifted evangelist, future missionary, or dynamic soul winner may be waiting for you to convey God's healing touch? Are you ready to find out?

> Dear brothers and sisters, if another believer is overcome by some sin, you who are godly should gently and humbly help that person back onto the right path. And be careful not to fall into the same temptation yourself. Share each other's burdens and in this way obey the law of Christ (Galatians 6:1, 2, NLT).

CHAPTER 6

Homemakers, fishermen, carpenters, soldiers, merchants, government servants, vinedressers, shepherds, shopkeepers, harvesters, builders, and many other commoners thronged to hear the ordinarily dressed Carpenter from Nazareth. Why? Without extravagant display, flowery oratory, or an impressive entourage, Jesus attracted varieties of peoples, but especially ordinary and everyday workers. Lacking royal patronage, political backing, a stunning wardrobe, and other accoutrements normally associated with successful people, this commonplace Galilean gathered an enormous following among those judged average, mundane, and normal. Disciples among the wealthier, aristocratic classes were seemingly invisible compared with these masses. What characteristics and qualities emerged through Jesus' message and lifestyle that enabled such effectiveness? What can twenty-first-century Christians emulate from Christ's pattern to reproduce that effectiveness today?

Identification

Christian missionaries have learned that cultural barriers are natural impediments against spreading the gospel message. Obviously language, the currency of thought, needs mastering to facilitate communication. This, however, formed only one of several significant barriers. Clothing, eating habits, leisure utilization, financial practices, family relationships, spiritual understanding, and dozens of interrelated lifestyle factors constitute additional hurdles.

Discipleship

The missionary classic *Peace Child* conveys the story of missionary Don Richardson, who struggled to find metaphors for communicating the gospel to primitive peoples. Famously, while presenting the passion narrative, his listeners laughed approvingly when Judas's betrayal was recounted. Within that culture, conspiracy and betrayal were considered virtuous! Had Richardson grown up within that culture, he probably would have avoided that memorable mistake. Cultural lifestyle characteristics are often shaped imperceptibly by numerous factors so subtle that this process happens unnoticed. Beginning in the womb, continuing at the playground, these characteristics are constantly being shaped around the dinner table, the classroom, and the workplace. Understandably, these attributes, like language, are more easily acquired by naturally growing into them rather than by someone adopting them later in life. Actually, adopting them might suggest phoniness, insincerity, or ulterior motives.

Heavenly wisdom selected Nazareth (an average location), Joseph and Mary (an ordinary blended family), and carpentry (a respectable but simple occupation) for Jesus' upbringing. Heaven's Royalty was born among cattle and sheep! Christ's contemporaries believed Him ordinary. His townspeople considered Him ordinary. "Everyone spoke well of him and was amazed by the gracious words that came from his lips. 'How can this be?' they asked. 'Isn't this Joseph's son?' " (Luke 4:22, NLT). Heaven purposely designed Christ's "ordinariness."

> The Son did not come to help angels; he came to help the descendants of Abraham. Therefore, it was necessary for him to be made in every respect like us, his brothers and sisters, so that he could be our merciful and faithful High Priest (Hebrews 2:16, 17, NLT).

Christ's humble upbringing facilitated His natural identification with common people. Jesus swallowed their cooking, sported their clothing, played their games, attended their weddings, gathered their stories, and completely identified Himself with everyday people. Had Christ enjoyed the advantages of royal palaces, abundant wealth, politically positioned relationships, and similar notions common people might have scorned Him and probably would have ignored Him. Instead, He was enthusiastically received as "one of ours." Having been born average, He had naturally acquired the tastes, habits, and feelings of the Jewish masses.

Rather than impeding Christ's mission, His upbringing propelled it forward. Every believer who considers himself or herself ordinary should contemplate the implications of this fact. How often have believers surrendered their calling to advance Christ's mission because they consider themselves unqualified, nonprofessional, and/or ordinary. This Christian caste theology depends on the official priesthood to forward God's kingdom, standing complacently along the sidelines either guiltily cheering or arrogantly complaining! "We're not trained for pastor's work." "We'll confuse people." "We're just an ordinary, run-of-the-mill church. Let seminary-trained ministers make disciples. Aren't they paid to accomplish that?"

Suppose that armies fought battles using this philosophy. Soldiers are deployed. Their mission is to rescue prisoners, dislodge entrenched enemies, and recapture lost territory. Before engaging their enemies, several foxhole conversations are overheard.

One private speaks with another: "We're not really needed here. We're ordinary privates equipped with rifles. Airplanes eradicate more enemies in seconds than foot soldiers destroy in months. Battleships also demonstrate incredible firepower. Tanks will dominate our enemies without our assistance. Let's be seated, swallow some MREs, and enjoy the show!"

Another private speaks, "Agreed. We're just ordinary privates anyway. Generals access detailed surveillance and classified intelligence. Colonels graduated from officer-training programs. Captains know tactical maneuvers and control sophisticated communications equipment. They're making whopping salaries. Shouldn't they be doing the fighting?"

Still another private expresses himself: "Exactly! With such an extensive mission, what possible difference could pitifully ordinary foot soldiers like us make? Who needs our little peashooters anyway?"

Somewhat agreeing, a captain chatters, "These lamebrain privates aren't producing. Winning battles with these idiots is tantamount to painting the capitol building with fingernail polish applicators. They're not postponing my promotion. I'll establish my competency without them. Bring on the battleships, airplanes, and tanks."

Not surprisingly, churches that utilize these tactics flounder. Those ordinary rifle-toting privates are indispensable. Accomplishing the mission is *impossible* without their enthusiastic participation. Often the ordinary church member enjoys tremendous advantages over the professionals in the disciple-making process.

Discipleship

1. Unbelievers frequently shun contact with religious professionals such as pastors. Sidestepping these professionals is relatively easy. Pastors occupy church buildings, busying themselves with church maintenance. So unbelievers avoid church buildings ("The building would collapse if I entered!") and the ministers cloistered there. Unbelievers, however, labor, purchase, vacation, and complete dozens of transactions in which they encounter ordinary Christians who are repairpersons, shopkeepers, government officials, salespeople, coaches, educators, cosmetologists, truck drivers, construction managers, nurses, electricians, plumbers, welders, therapists, miners, automotive mechanics, and so forth. Ordinary Christians have them surrounded! Pastors will never reach all these people. Ordinary Christians can.

2. Many people cannot identify with professional ministers because of misconceptions about righteousness. Ministers are viewed as separated from reality. "They could never understand my trials, temptations, and tribulations. They're in the holiness business. They'll never understand my sin-filled mistake-prone life." They, nevertheless, can identify with their Christian coworkers, based upon their mutual occupation and, perhaps, mutual interests. After all, the believer and unbeliever alike are hairdressers, mechanics, cooks, crane operators, steamfitters, farmers, painters, or tellers. Anyone working beside them cannot be all that weird. Their children may share the same Little League baseball team. They may appreciate the same leisure activities such as fishing, golfing, or bowling. They may enjoy the same restaurants. Friendships are formed, bridging the chasm that separates believer from unbeliever.

3. Unfortunately, recent sexual and financial scandals involving church professionals have created other barriers between clergypersons and unbelievers. While grace-oriented Christians may forgive these moral lapses, many unbelievers latch on to these incidents with self-justification. "They're no better than us sinners anyway. Who needs religion? We're just as good as anybody else without the hassle." Ministry professionals seldom penetrate hearts this extremely biased. They are considered hypocrites simply because they are ministers. Ordinary Christians, once again, have enormous advantages. Fortunately unbelievers cannot completely avoid Christians forever. When believers offer encouraging words, listening ears, and occasionally financial support, lasting impressions are made. Prejudices are gradually melted. As windshield cracks keep extending millimeter by millimeter, so Christian kindness keeps extending and compromises the barrier against God's Spirit. Christian professionals seldom have opportunities to impress these closed minds. Ordinary Christians encounter them daily.

Jesus reached ordinary people who could not identify with the priesthood, the Pharisees, or the Sadducees. They could identify with Christ because this Carpenter, sometime Fisherman, and modestly dressed fellow Laborer walked alongside them. Identification with the masses enabled Christ to penetrate hardened hearts with the gospel message. Dedicated disciple-makers will not overlook this important first step.

Industrious study

Identification alone is insufficient. While this forms the irreplaceable foundation for additional contact with unbelievers, just working alongside them will seldom interest them in the gospel. Jesus carefully studied those He invited into His kingdom. So thoroughly did He know the Samaritan woman that she exclaimed, "Come and see a man who told me everything I ever did!" (John 4:29, NLT). When Jesus described Nathanael, Nathanael questioned, "How do you know about me?" (John 1:48, NLT). The term *industrious* indicates hard working, conscientious, energetic, diligence. This characterized Jesus' approach to disciple-making. *Hard-working* suggests, accurately, that authentic disciple-making does not occur easily or spontaneously.

Biologically, the notion of spontaneous generation—that life just mysteriously, even accidentally, happens—was jettisoned years ago. Perhaps daydreams of spontaneous conversions should now be rejected also. Knowing people's interests, desires, dreams, nightmares, disappointments, triumphs, and characteristics requires work. This is rewarding, enjoyable labor; but it is work. Rather than being accidental or spontaneous, it is intentionally focused. Some practical observations might include the following: (1) Why is this person timid or gregarious? (2) What are the passions that drive this person's decisions and actions? (3) What can be ascertained regarding this person's character traits, personality, and aspirations? (4) How might family relationships influence this person's choices? Remember that family may include influential friends and biological relationships. (5) How does this person relate to financial matters? (6) What is this person's religious or spiritual background? (7) What does this person understand to be his or her central purpose? Obviously, the list could be extended. The primary point is that active disciple-makers must intentionally focus their attention on those factors that influence spiritual decision-making.

Conscientious suggests that spiritual integrity undergirds the process completely. Numerous accounts underscore the dangers involved in knowing other people thoroughly when integrity is absent. Unworthy counselors, including some pastors, have utilized such extensive knowledge for self-serving purposes leading to sexual compromise or financial greed. Conscientious study, however, is guided only by the sincere desire to glorify God and guide souls into His kingdom.

Energetic implies enthusiasm. The word *enthusiasm* is derived from two Greek words, *en* and *theos,* meaning, "in God." Divine energy, capable of overcoming every obstacle and lifting downtrodden spirits, is offered "in God." Apprenticeship in divine kingdom building demands nothing less. One employer once addressed his employees with these words: "Those employees who are not fired with enthusiasm will be fired—with enthusiasm!" Genuine believers are fired up about soul winning. Divine energy and excitement accompany those who would lead others into a saving relationship with Jesus.

Diligence indicates persistence or perseverance—that quality which never gives up. It is Winston Churchill refusing to surrender his country without a fight. It is Martin Luther King Jr. marching for equality although it cost him his life. It is General MacArthur refusing to accept defeat in retaking the Philippines. In one of the most memorable moments in summer Olympic history, Derek Redmond, the British four-hundred-meter record holder, entered the semifinal heat of the 1992 Barcelona Olympics with the opportunity to represent his country in the Olympic final. Unfortunately, he pulled his hamstring during the race and crumbled to the pavement. Stretcher bearers rushed to help him, but Redmond refused. Eluding security guards Redmond's father, Jim, leaped from the stands onto the track. Reportedly, the elder Redmond told his son, "Son, you don't have to finish the race," to which the younger Redmond responded, "Yes, I do." Arm in arm they hobbled around the track to the finish line. All across the stadium those who were not wiping tears from their eyes were giving the injured sprinter and his father a standing ovation.

That diligence characterizes every believer's attitude regarding the work of leading people to Christ. Paul writes, "All athletes are disciplined in their training. They do it to win a prize that will fade away, but we do it for an eternal prize" (1 Corinthians 9:25, NLT). Derek Redmond was so dedicated to the ideals of his sport that he endured the pain to finish the race. May every believer be so dedicated to God's kingdom and the divine call to make disciples from every nation that we will exercise that same diligence in our lives.

Irrepressible expression

Not only did Jesus identify with ordinary people and study their lives industriously, He irrepressibly expressed the gospel utilizing familiar stories and recognizable metaphors. In which gospel have we read those oft-repeated words, "Well, I didn't really say anything because I didn't want to be overly aggressive or offensive?" Apparently, the biblical writers never caught Jesus excusing Himself like that. Then why should those claiming to be Christ's followers state this repeatedly? How frequently have we heard, "We'll just live good lives, be friendly neighbors, share some bread, and gather their mail while they're vacationing. They'll notice that we're believers. Should they desire more information, they'll surely ask questions"? Whenever potential disciples identified with Jesus, the Savior carefully studied their backgrounds and demeanor. Inevitably, He presented the gospel message verbally.

Suppose scientists developed automobiles that utilized water for fuel. These vehicles were shipped nationwide to licensed distributors. Their salespeople, however, evidenced a laissez-faire attitude. Rather than actively promoting this unique technological advancement, they adopted a passive approach. They cleaned, vacuumed, and polished their vehicles religiously. The showroom glass was immaculately kept, and the showroom floors shone spick-and-span. Even bathrooms were shipshape. Outside, flowers were watered generously and sidewalks were spotless. Salespeople prided themselves regarding their hygienic, sanitary, uncontaminated, unadulterated, wholesome environment. Beautiful showroom music piped through perfectly balanced speakers. Sparkling water flowed from their fountain. Salespeople dressed impeccably.

But their marquee remained vacant. No announcements regarding the miracle vehicles appeared. They utilized unconventional advertising methodology: they did none. When potential buyers accidentally wandered into the showroom, salespeople reclined comfortably, making virtually no effort to approach them. They reasoned, "We shouldn't be overly aggressive or offensive. That might drive them away. We've polished the outside meticulously, vacuumed the inside slavishly, and distributed bread hospitably without charge. Surely they'll notice our superior products. Should they desire more information they'll surely ask questions."

Actually, every 997th potential customer troubled themselves and awakened some snoring salesperson who dutifully directed them to the district sales manager. Rarely, the manager was available. These visits proved fruitful and infrequently sales were transacted. That delighted customer celebrated the wonder of water. Monthly sales reports were forwarded to regional sales managers, who faithfully collected data until the dealership finally declared bankruptcy. Unemployed salespeople wondered how such outstanding products failed to move rapidly.

Several blocks over, Bobby's Reconditioned Automobile Center marketed older gas-guzzling contraptions. Bobby's technicians worked diligently but obviously could not deliver products comparable with those available from new car dealerships. Nevertheless, Bobby's salespeople were energetic, shrewd, and unapologetically aggressive. Their enthusiasm boiled over faster than unwatched oatmeal. Whenever potential customers, enticed by classified advertisements and marquee-announced bargains, arrived, Bobby's salespeople greeted them, smiling, within thirty seconds. Salespeople extolled the virtues of their automobiles. "Classic" supplanted "outdated." "Delayed payment options" replaced "reduced interest rates."

Despite these obvious handicaps, Bobby's salespeople radiated warmth, listened attentively to their customers' desires and concerns, and provided pertinent information about their products. Sales skyrocketed. Unfortunately such sales facilitated skyrocketing gasoline prices because increased consumption (gas-guzzlers, remember?) forced petroleum shortages, which forced increased fuel charges (ethanol notwithstanding). Subsequently warfare erupted over control of the oilfields, destroying millions of young lives, causing international bankruptcies, and impoverishing the remaining inhabitants. If only Bobby's sales philosophy had motivated the other dealership's salespeople.

Christ realized, better than anyone, the consequences of bypassing spiritual opportunities. He aggressively expressed the gospel message with words. Failure in doing this meant spiritual disasters for individuals and horrific consequences for societies. *Aggressive* means neither antagonistic nor boisterous. Violence and belligerence are likewise excluded. *Aggressive* does mean assertive and determined. Firemen clearing a house are insistent, uncompromising, and sometimes forceful. Prayerfully guided by God's Holy Spirit, believers can present the gospel aggressively because the force lies not in the loudness of the presentation but is inherent to the powerful nature of Scripture and dependent upon the Spirit's inner working.

Remember, perfect love banishes all intimidation. Whenever believers, motivated by Christ's uncompromised love, communicate their faith, threats of personal rejection become secondary to God's mission of saving lost people. The Samaritan woman initially sidestepped Christ's invitation to spiritual life but was converted. Nicodemus evaded Jesus' probing questions, seemingly eternally lost. Nonetheless, years later, that spiritual seed planted in nighttime obscurity blossomed publicly and eternally.

Unfortunately, not everyone yielded their lives. The wealthy young aristocrat sorrowfully rejected Christ's invitation, but this could not discourage Christ from inviting others. Jesus irrepressibly expressed the gospel, outcomes notwithstanding. Ordinary twenty-first-century believers consumed with reaching their neighbors, friends, and relatives will certainly follow His example.

CHAPTER 7

Mackenzie lived within spitting distance of the state's penitentiary. Housing was substandard and undesirable. Employed neighbors purchased transparent plastic sheeting for covering windows during the frigid wintertime. Summertime brought nearly unbearable heat. Leaking rooftops; grassless backyards complemented by curbside junkyards; broken fences separating vacant, boarded-up houses; rusting windowless vehicles supported by flattened tires completed the picture. While other Christian retirees contented themselves by contributing towards overseas missions, two believers accepted God's calling to this penitentiary mission field. These ladies initiated the first Vacation Bible School for the neighborhood. Attendance was overwhelming, so they continued the ministry with a weekly story-time outreach.

Their attendees lacked Christian upbringing, church manners, cultured language, and similar niceties. Several children resided near the penitentiary precisely because their fathers were incarcerated within. Other families simply lacked sufficient financial resources to afford anything better. Accordingly, many children arrived unkempt, sullied, with running noses and hungry stomachs. Single indigent mothers were frankly attracted by this free babysitting with occasional feeding. The organizers were not deterred. Rather, they recruited another retired volunteer who roamed the neighborhood, loading busload after busload (sometimes totaling 150 children) for an occasional Sunday adventure at the church's youth center. The children enjoyed peanut butter-and-jelly

Chapter 7

sandwiches, juice, cookies, games, roller-skating, and carnival rides.

Mackenzie began attending story time and associated activities with her younger brothers, replacement diapers securely tucked beneath their little arms. The middle-school-aged adolescent served these younger siblings as their caregiver and protector because their mother worked incessantly, providing basic necessities for themselves and their jobless (unemployable?) stepfather. Nevertheless, Mackenzie attended weekly, faithfully bringing her younger brothers along. Schoolmates remember Mackenzie as always smiling and cheerful. They likewise recollect that she was overweight, wearing outdated blouses featuring high collars. Initially one schoolmate asked her grandmother, the ministry leader, why Mackenzie dressed poorly, thinking the cause was either fashion ignorance or poverty. She learned the actual motivation: concealment.

Those collars and loose blouses shrouded bruises and rope burns inflicted by Mackenzie's stepfather. Sometime later, Mackenzie's younger brother arrived for church with his broken leg in a cast. Officially they claimed, "It was a simple accident." Several weeks later, he stopped attending services. Parishioners learned that Roderick's stepfather had become impatient with his complaints about itching. Heating a metallic coat hanger he rammed it inside the cast, embedding it underneath his skin. Naturally, Mackenzie greatly feared her stepfather. Having reached feminine maturity, she nightly secured her bedroom entrance to avoid continual sexual assaults. Things worsened. Incompetent authorities refused action. Desperate, Mackenzie attempted suicide, overdosing on prescription medication. Finally, the authorities listened, placing her in foster care when she recovered.

Mackenzie's adoptive family provided normalcy and financed her enrollment in a Christian high school that their daughter attended. Finally, her Christian baptismal commitment was supported rather than undermined. She flourished within her new environment and quickly established new friendships. After secondary-school graduation, she attended college, graduating from the nursing program. Twenty-five years later, Mackenzie Williamson is happily married, having relocated to another state. She regularly volunteers as a nurse for Christian summer camp programs and sends her daughter to another Christian high school, where she sings with the traveling choir.

Those retired grandmothers who tirelessly sacrificed for Mackenzie and hundreds of other children have long since passed away. Their spiritual investment, however, continues returning living dividends generation after generation. Following other retirees, they might have invested all their time gardening, vacationing, shopping, and so forth; instead, they selflessly embraced grubby, abandoned, outcast children and became God's transformational agents in the penitentiary's shadow.

> "For I was hungry, and you fed me. I was thirsty, and you gave me a drink. I was a stranger, and you invited me into your home. I was naked, and you gave me clothing. I was sick, and you cared for me. I was in prison, and you visited me" (Matthew 25:35, 36, NLT).

These well-known words, echoing throughout the intervening centuries, validate Christian ministry among the disenfranchised today. Christ's wording strongly suggests that eternal consequences hinge upon the believer's response to needy, undesirable, societal outcasts. This response essentially ministers to Christ Himself.

Modern society produces many outcasts. There are *moral* outcasts. These people have consciously embraced self-destructive practices. Those practices destroy others' lives also. Substance abusers, prostitutes, cocaine traffickers, pedophiles, career criminals, pornographers, alcoholics, and other like-minded associates populate this category. Unfortunately, families, especially children, are similarly shunned by polite society because they are associated with these moral outcasts. The adult child of one notorious pornographer, addressing a Christian college assembly, lamented the shame she experienced during childhood because schoolmates shunned her since they associated her with her father's nefarious activities.

There are also *social* outcasts. Somehow every society divides insiders from outsiders. Sometimes societies function with official caste designations, while others create unofficial but nevertheless tangible distinctions. American history demonstrates the fallacy of the melting pot. First generation immigrants were generally separated from the indigenous population until generations of intermarriage softened ethnic distinctions and animosities. Once absorbed into the new indigenous population, the former outsiders, having become insiders, discriminated against newer immigrant populations. Financial standing oftentimes separated outsiders from insiders. Thus, ethnicity and poverty have created outcast populations whose members have contributed nothing toward their exclusion.

There are *behavioral* outcasts. Milder expressions of this phenomenon would include loners, geeks, nerds, wallflowers, alongside others whose childhood behaviors position them outside mainstream participation. They commonly eschew varsity athletics, cheerleading squads, campus politics, academic competitions, and similar social involvement. Characterized by social powerlessness, lacking secure social networks ("belonging"), such persons frequently withdraw from broader society, sometimes forming negatively focused alternative social networks. Extreme examples might include Goths: they are typically teenagers whose bizarre dress includes blackened, heavily applied eyeliner and fingernail polish, dramatically styled black clothing, tattoos, and unusual, generally black hairstyles. Other behavioral outcasts include patients suffering from various mental illnesses. Sometimes these are genetically caused, but growing numbers have environmental causes. Post-traumatic stress disorder reflects the increasing violence experienced throughout modern society, particularly in battlefields. Terminology that includes *manic-depressive disorder* and *schizophrenic* has become commonplace. Oftentimes mental illnesses are accompanied by homelessness, hunger, and smelliness, further driving these sufferers away from mainstream lifestyles and ordinary socialization.

Christ died to save these moral, social, and behavioral outcasts. Jesus' commissioning includes empowering disciples to disseminate God's transforming message among society's fringe peoples. Jesus loves them, so should we.

Ministry to moral outcasts

Eventually he [Jesus] came to the Samaritan village of Sychar, near the field that Jacob gave to his son Joseph. Jacob's well was there; and Jesus, tired from the long walk, sat wearily beside the well about noontime. Soon a Samaritan woman came to draw water, and Jesus said to her, "Please give me a drink." He was alone at the time because his disciples had gone into the village to buy some food.

The woman was surprised, for Jews refuse to have anything to do with Samaritans. She said to Jesus, "You are a Jew, and I am a Samaritan woman. Why are you asking me for a drink?"

Jesus replied, "If you only knew the gift God has for you and who you are speaking to, you would ask me, and I would give you living water."

"But sir, you don't have a rope or a bucket," she said, "and this well is very deep. Where would you get this living water? And besides, do you think you're greater than our ancestor Jacob, who gave us this well? How can you offer better water than he and his sons and his animals enjoyed?"

Jesus replied, "Anyone who drinks this water will soon become thirsty again. But those who drink the water I give will never be thirsty again. It becomes a fresh, bubbling spring within them, giving them eternal life."

"Please, sir," the woman said, "give me this water! Then I'll never be thirsty again, and I won't have to come here to get water."

"Go and get your husband," Jesus told her.

"I don't have a husband," the woman replied.

Jesus said, "You're right! You don't have a husband—for you have had five husbands, and you aren't married to the man you're living with now. You certainly spoke the truth!" (John 4:5–18, NLT).

This Samaritan woman approached Jacob's well during the midday heat, whereas most women obtained water during cooler morning hours. This strongly suggests she was avoiding contact with other townspeople. Probably attractive enough to excite jealousy among potential rivals, she knew that her moral failures provided sufficient ammunition for gossipers and talebearers alike. Whose husband might she subsequently seduce? Her multiple marriages and unnumbered liaisons—subject matter supplemented by lavish imaginations and sensational speculation—created almost unlimited conversational material.

Family protection, community appearances, and similar righteous concerns seemingly justified the townspeople's ongoing castigation of this woman. Shockingly, One absolutely righteous, completely knowledgeable regarding her transgressions, oversteps ethnic, social, and gender barriers, engaging her in conversation. Although surprised, possibly questioning His motives, she responds. Christ's sequence provides the pattern that every disciple-maker should understand.

First, utilizing the metaphor of living water, He provides spiritual motivation. Lying dormant within every straying soul, God's Spirit has implanted aspirations toward wholeness, spiritual adventure, and eternal commitment. Until these aspirations are awakened, moral rectitude is impossible. Sermonizing, criticizing, finger-pointing, and similar tactics actually harden people, cementing them within their moral failures. Elsewhere, Christ cautioned that expelling demonic forces without immediately supplanting them with righteousness would eventually produce magnified failures. Jesus' methodology places horse before wagon. The indwelling Divine Spirit necessarily precedes lifestyle changes. Correcting immoral living, without primarily introducing spiritual transformation, produces short-term changes or long-term legalism. Shame, guilt, and apprehension supply short-term motivation; however, self-destructive behavior demonstrates the powerlessness of these forces to facilitate long-term conversion. Before confronting this Samaritan regarding her immoral lifestyle, Christ invites her to explore and experience spiritual life.

Second, Christ does expect lifestyle changes. Authentic Christianity demands righteousness. Cheap, self-excusing grace finds no foundation within Jesus' teachings. Genuine Christianity does not have revolving doors, constantly swinging believers between rebellious worldly living and contrite confession. Conversion's fruitage is demonstrated through changed lives.

Third, conversion always culminates with recognition and acknowledgement of the unsung Nazarene as the everlasting Messiah. Humanity's helplessness is rescued by the Eternal Deliverer. What weakened humans are incapable of accomplishing themselves, Christ achieved through divine deliverance. Christ first awakens spiritual aspirations; next, He compares our current spiritual condition with those aspirations, and then He supplies Himself as the reconciliation that alone overcomes despair and establishes His righteousness. To approach moral outcasts apart from Christ's sequence foreshadows inevitable failure.

Or think about this modern story. Marissa was approaching sixteen. Although she was young, life experiences had chiseled somberness across her countenance. Listening to a nationally syndicated Christian broadcast, she gathered glimmers of hope. Subsequently she penned her personal story and shared it with the broadcast.

When she was twelve, her mother's drunken, abusive boyfriend had evicted her because she rebuffed his sexual overtures. With her exceptional beauty and a mature woman's figure, she appeared closer to eighteen than thirteen. Naturally, older men considered her attractive and willingly offered this homeless teenager their assistance, including lodging.

Pregnancy, delivery, and motherhood quickly followed. She soon discovered that her "benefactor" loathed crying infants and, approaching fourteen, she was again evicted. Other men followed, and she got pregnant again.

Social service agencies were understandably concerned about this young mother's parenting inabilities, the toddler's physical welfare and upbringing, especially because of the second pregnancy. An experienced social worker was dispatched to retrieve the toddler. That child represented the only authentic affection Marissa had ever experienced. Everyone else lusted after her, but this child genuinely loved her. Should she finally be deprived of this singular love? Desperation overwhelmed Marissa. Determination to defend herself displaced rational thinking. When the social worker arrived, Marissa killed her.

During Marissa's incarceration, while sharing her tragic narrative with the broadcast, she exclaimed, "I ain't loved by nobody! I need somebody to love me. I need a father, a mother, and a husband. Can somebody please help me?" While Marissa awaited sentencing, the broadcast dispatched a representative who told her that God loved her regardless of circumstances. That lonely teenager, facing possibly lifetime incarceration, acknowledged the divine provision of salvation, accepted Calvary's unlimited love, and became a baptized believer.

Fifteen years later, a recruiter for a Christian college was answering questions about his school for a family that attended church in Marissa's hometown. Having visited Marissa in prison years earlier as the broadcast's representative, he realized that their church was the same one Marissa knew from their prison outreach. He asked about her, and learned that the family was familiar with her story. In fact, her teenage children were active attendees at their church. God's people had embraced one unloved outcast teenager with compassionate, nonjudgmental friendship and snatched her family from Satan's clutches.

Or, here's another true story. Franklin had been incarcerated for half his life when he was released from prison. This murderer began attending evangelistic meetings in a small countryside church. During the meetings, he surrendered his life to Christ, subsequently was baptized and joined the church fellowship. The church membership, primarily populated by women, was necessarily cautious about this balding, muscular stranger with the penetrating stare. Franklin's decisions oftentimes caused consternation. For financial reasons, he established residence in a local bar's apartment as the nighttime security. His acquaintances differed significantly from the usual church crowd. Some mannerisms betrayed his years of incarceration.

The congregation was, however, loving, accepting, and supportive. Seeing beyond Franklin's rough exterior, as Christ had done with the Gerasene demoniacs, prostitutes, and other societal outcasts, the countryside church encouraged his spiritual transformation. Franklin's parole violations (not for additional criminal activity) caused him to go back to prison. During this period, he continued correspondence with his pastor. The profoundness of his conversion was revealed through those letters.

Franklin's elderly father lived with his daughter, Franklin's sister, in an isolated house. Four youthful brigands invaded the house, killing Franklin's defenseless father during the robbery. They escaped with twenty dollars. When Franklin's pastor read the letter, his emotions overflowed. Having enjoyed an intimate relationship with his own father, knowing that Franklin had experienced a similar relationship with his, and recognizing the senseless violence against this helpless individual, the pastor expected to read expressions of hatred and revenge.

Would this one-time murderer not threaten vengeance for such heinous crimes? Would he not desire unmitigated justice? Instead Franklin requested prayers that these youthful murderers would find repentance, forgiveness, and everlasting life. The always-loving Savior had embraced him, a seemingly insignificant church fellowship had accepted him, and now his supreme desire was reaching these criminal outcasts who had egregiously wronged him. Although imprisoned, Franklin enjoyed spiritual freedoms few others experience. Another outcast had been liberated through divine compassion dispersed through loving believers.

Ministry to social outcasts

And I saw another angel flying through the sky, carrying the eternal Good News to proclaim to the people who belong to this world—to every nation, tribe, language, and people (Revelation 14:6 NLT).

"My Temple will be called a house of prayer for all nations.

For the Sovereign Lord,
    who brings back the outcasts of Israel, says:
I will bring others, too,
    besides my people Israel" (Isaiah 56:7, 8, NLT).

Dear brothers and sisters, how can you claim to have faith in our glorious Lord Jesus Christ if you favor some people over others (James 2:1, NLT).

A Canaanite woman from that vicinity came to him, crying out, "Lord, Son of David, have mercy on me! My daughter is demon-possessed and suffering terribly." . . . He answered, "I was sent only to the lost sheep of Israel." The woman came and knelt before him, "Lord, help me!" she said. He replied, "It is not right to take the children's bread and toss it to the dogs." "Yes it is, Lord," she said. "Even dogs eat the crumbs that fall from their master's table." Then Jesus said to her, "Woman, you have great faith! Your request is granted" (Matthew 15:22, 24–28, TNIV).

Racism is a terrible sin. Moral outcasts have predetermined their status by their choices. Behavioral outcasts might possibly alter their perception by changing. Social outcasts, however, are stereotyped regardless of character and pigeonholed according to preconceived ideas. Sometimes national customs formalize this situation—for example, caste systems or apartheid—but frequently this prejudicial attitude is expressed informally. Unfortunately, culture's prevailing prejudices are sanctioned and sometimes furthered by the church. This regrettable reality must be reversed. Courageous confrontation rather than quiet acquiescence will characterize the genuinely converted. Scriptural principles present one unifying message that totally transcends man-made barriers.

When Jesus' disciples encouraged dismissing the Syrophoencian (Canaanite) woman, Christ refused compliance. Quoting one well-known aphorism about puppies, children, and their food, the Messiah challenged her faith. Rather than feeling rebuffed, she reconfigured the aphorism, recognizing Christ's invitation to faith. God's "crumbs" were more than sufficient for restoring her daughter. That episode reminded the disciples that Heaven's bounties are available to every individual who expresses faith regardless of ethnic or racial backgrounds.

Consequently, you are no longer foreigners and strangers, but fellow citizens with God's people and also members of his household, built upon the foundation of the apostles and prophets, with Christ Jesus himself as the chief cornerstone (Ephesians 2:19, TNIV).

Ministry to behavioral outcasts

Daily headlines highlight multiple shooting sprees scattered across the United States. Regrettably, weaponry gathers attention and debate, though the human suffering that spawned these brutal attacks seems minimized. What causes that emptiness, isolation, and depression that makes attention-grabbing violence desirable? What should believers, individually and corporately, be doing to create societies where everybody senses belonging, purpose, acceptance, and appreciation?

Creating such opportunities forestalls the development of behavioral outcasts and offers reconciliation for those who already consider themselves outsiders. Providing appropriate appreciation and recognition for everybody presupposes widespread awareness of various talents and abilities. Why should students be worshiped because they can shoot balls through iron cylinders while painters and artists are overlooked? Why should musical performances be applauded while the kindness and Christian service of other students goes unrecognized? Why should society reward physical beauty while ignoring unselfish character? Ministering to behavioral outcasts means getting priorities straight.

Secondly, such ministry involves taking risks. Would Christ think, "They're absolutely weird; that bizarre clothing doesn't belong in church; their sailor's language is filthy, uncouth, and totally unacceptable; they obviously haven't used deodorant in several months; let's locate some upstanding citizens and evangelize them instead"? Hardly.

Neither should believers. *Our* behaviors are likewise filthy rags apart from Christ. Although they are battered and unappreciated, having complicated their lives with undesirable choices, Christ still loves them. His sacrificial death reconciles their rebelliousness, providing atonement for their sinfulness. Risking involvement with outcasts seldom brings immediate satisfaction. Nevertheless, over time, disciple-makers have found their efforts richly rewarding. Millions of Mackenzies, Marissas, and Franklins await our witness. Why should we keep them waiting?

CHAPTER 8

"One day a prospecting party, penetrating far into the Klondike, came upon a miner's hut. Entering the hut, they found the frozen bodies of two men and a large quantity of gold. On a table there was a letter which told of the successful search for the precious ore. In their eagerness to mine the gold, the miners had neglected to make provision for the coming winter. Each day the two men found gold in abundance. One morning they awoke and saw that a blizzard had come. For days the tempest raged. All hope of escape left when their little store of food was gone. They wrote the letter and lay down in the midst of abounding gold."[1]

How well this narrative illustrates the spiritual condition of millions of wealthy people whose pursuits have resulted in personal emptiness. Jesus asked, "What advantages would worldly wealth provide should the wealthy suffer eternal loss?" Jesus treasured wealthy people as much as He valued people within His own socioeconomic class. Jesus, the ordinary everyday Carpenter, was neither intimidated nor enamored by worldly wealth. Jesus must have known well the challenges of supporting a family by the work of one's hands, yet He exhibited no jealousy regarding wealthy people. Prosperous people, politically positioned people, could not intimidate Jesus either. "Then one of the temple guards standing nearby slapped Jesus across the face. 'Is that the way to answer the high priest?' he demanded. Jesus replied, 'If I said anything wrong, you must prove it. But if I'm speaking the truth, why are you beating me?' "

(John 18:22, 23, NLT). Unlike Christ, many contemporary Christians are either enamored or intimidated by the wealthy, an attitude that cripples their witness to the wealthy.

How did Jesus, born of humble parentage, self-educated rather than formally schooled, tradesman rather than aristocrat, effectively minister among affluent people?

First, Jesus remembered His heavenly position. The story is told of an elderly indigent couple that always walked with courtly dignity. Observers wondered what might explain their dignified mannerisms. Inquiry regarding their background resolved their puzzlement. Observers discovered that they were lineal descendants of court nobility. This explained their courtly appearance and dignified bearing, adverse circumstances notwithstanding. Jesus, likewise, remembered His heavenly lineage. Although a carpenter below, He was royalty above. *His* heavenly Father distributed all wealth. Everything ultimately belonged to Him. This heavenly perspective during Christ's earthly sojourn essentially vaccinated Jesus against monetary diseases.

Wealth meant nothing to Jesus. Being God's royal Offspring, Christ had owned everything already. The wealthiest aristocrat's belongings were peanuts compared with His Father's holdings. Why should these earthly playthings intimidate anyone? What are glittering lights to the universe's Architect? What are yachts to the ocean's Creator? What are earthly mansions compared with heavenly palaces? Owning multiple constellations would barely qualify to occupy the outskirts of God's neighborhood. The most prosperous potentate was peasant class compared with the lowliest heavenly angel. Nebuchadnezzar, Alexander, and Augustus failed to completely subdue measly planet Earth, yet were considered among humanity's wealthiest. How did puppet royalty (Herod), provincial governors (Pilate), and religious scalawags (Caiaphas) think they could intimidate the divine Messiah?

Christians should likewise remember their heavenly position.

You will know the confidence that he calls you to have and the glorious wealth that God's people will inherit. You will also know the unlimited greatness of his power as it works might and strength for us, the believers (Ephesians 1:18, 19, GOD'S WORD).

You are no longer foreigners and outsiders but citizens

together with God's people and members of God's family. You are built on the foundation of the apostles and prophets. Christ Jesus himself is the cornerstone (Ephesians 2:19, 20, God's Word).

However, you are chosen people, a royal priesthood, a holy nation, people who belong to God. You were chosen to tell about the excellent qualities of God, who called you out of darkness into his marvelous light (1 Peter 2:9, God's Word).

Whenever God's chosen people recognize their exalted position through Jesus the Messiah, the world's wealthy cannot intimidate them. Heavenly standing trumps worldly possessions every time. Speaking God's message to employers, financiers, well-to-do neighbors, wealthy schoolmates, or politically powerful people should elicit no greater apprehension than would sharing Christ with poorer classes. Heavenly ambassadors should not feel compelled to apologize because divine dispatch trumps everything else.

Little children shall lead! "Aramaeans brought back as a captive from the land of Israel a little girl, who became a servant to Naaman's wife. She said to her mistress, 'If only my master could meet the prophet who lives in Samaria'" (2 Kings 5:2, 3, NEB). Although enslaved, this youngster directed her captors toward physical healing through Elisha, Yahweh's prophet. Separated from her family, she was youthful and a member of the lowest caste. Nevertheless, Naaman listened, accepted this nameless child's advice, and experienced physical and spiritual deliverance. Older people, intimidated by Naaman's wealth and position, might have maintained silence. They might have reasoned that someone that wealthy would never have listened to slaves. They might have conjectured that Naaman's problem was not theirs anyway. Perhaps their resentment might have caused them to surreptitiously applaud his demise. Nonetheless, this unnamed maiden etched her heroic endeavor into scriptural history, demonstrating for every generation that even the humblest sincere believer possesses unfettered abilities to reach the wealthiest classes.

Next, Jesus recognized spiritual poverty. Material wealth frequently disguises spiritual destitution. Jesus once admonished a youthful aristocratic follower, "Sell all that you possess, and distribute it to the poor, and you shall have treasure in heaven" (Luke 18:22, NASB). Jesus clearly understood that possessions commonly spawned possessiveness and occasionally provoked materialistic possession (cf. demonic possession). Ancient wisdom declares,

> "Grant me neither poverty nor riches; feed me my portion of nourishment, lest I be full and deny Thee and say, 'Who is the LORD?' or lest I be poor, and steal, and violate God's name" (Proverbs 30:8, 9, MLB).

Yet people still reverence accumulation, enlargement, and hoarding. This philosophy was foreshadowed by Jesus' teaching narrative regarding wealth:

> "Beware! Guard against every kind of greed. Life is not measured by how much you own."
> Then he told them a story: "A rich man had a fertile farm that produced fine crops. He said to himself, 'What should I do? I don't have room for all my crops.' Then he said, 'I know! I'll tear down my barns and build bigger ones. Then I'll have room enough to store all my wheat and other goods. And I'll sit back and say to myself, "My friend, you have enough stored away for years to come. Now take it easy! Eat, drink, and be merry!" '
> "But God said to him, 'You fool! You will die this very night. Then who will get everything you worked for?'
> "Yes, a person is a fool to store up earthly wealth but not have a rich relationship with God" (Luke 12:15–21, NLT).

Jesus realized that extremely wealthy people sometimes camouflaged their spiritual desperation with pleasure seeking, materialism, and frivolous entertainments. Penetrating their masquerades, He exposed their spiritual wounds and offered healing. Christ neither sidestepped such confrontation nor sugarcoated His vocabulary. Although tactful and compassionate, He recognized that spiritual cancer requires treatment. Ignoring problems does not facilitate treatment.

Suppose you visited a renowned physician because you suffered a backache. His diagnosis reveals that kidney cancer is the cause. Rather than informing you, however, he avoids the matter, choosing to discuss politics, sporting events, and your favorite hobby. Your specialist prescribes some common pain medication and suggests that things will gradually improve. Your pharmacist fills your prescription, and some temporary relief follows. The cancerous tumor, however, continues to grow. Left untreated it metastasizes, attacking organs, nerves, and your skeletal system. Your condition rapidly deteriorates until death mercifully overtakes you. In retrospect, would you have preferred the truth coupled with, perhaps, painful but effective treatment, or would you have selected pleasant conversation that would not acknowledge the problem? Obviously, you would have preferred the truth.

Jesus declares truth. "You say, 'I am rich. I have everything I want. I don't need a thing!' And you don't realize that you are wretched and miserable and poor and blind and naked" (Revelation 3:17, NLT). These words were prefaced with a promise to spit out these distasteful pretenders. Actually, "spit" somewhat sanitizes the English reading. The Greek ἐμέσαι literally denotes "vomiting" rather than "spitting." God cannot stand avariciousness. God would rather throw up.

Because Christ loves wealthy people, He refuses to withhold truth even when that means calling them wretched and miserable. Remember this famous example?

> Zacchaeus quickly climbed down and took Jesus to his house in great excitement and joy.
>
> But the people were displeased. "He has gone to be the guest of a notorious sinner," they grumbled.
>
> Meanwhile, Zacchaeus stood before the Lord and said, "I will give half of my wealth to the poor, Lord, and if I have cheated people on their taxes, I will give them back four times as much!"
>
> Jesus responded, "Salvation has come to this home today, for this man has shown himself to be a true son of Abraham. For the Son of Man came to seek and save those who are lost" (Luke 19:6–10, NLT).

The heavenly Physician diagnoses greediness, confronts greedy people, and provides the incomparable cure. Christ's followers *must* follow suit. Paul certainly does.

Paul, writing Timothy, says,

But people who long to be rich fall into temptation and are trapped by many foolish and harmful desires that plunge them into ruin and destruction. For the love of money is the root of all kinds of evil. And some people, craving money, have wandered from the true faith and pierced themselves with many sorrows. . . .

Teach those who are rich in this world not to be proud and not to trust in their money, which is so unreliable. Their trust should be in God, who richly gives us all that we need for our enjoyment. Tell them to use their money to do good. They should be rich in good works and generous to those in need, always being ready to share with others. By doing this they will be storing up their treasure as a good foundation for the future so that they may experience true life (1 Timothy 6:9, 10, 17–19, NLT).

Paul instructs Timothy to boldly admonish wealthy people regarding their spiritual condition, although Timothy was undoubtedly not wealthy himself. Rather than fearing prosperous people based upon feelings of inferiority, Timothy was installed as their spiritual professor. His spiritual treasures outweighed and outranked their material possessions. This principle applies equally to contemporary Christians. They are called to recognize spiritual poverty, communicate the diagnosis tactfully without regarding the person's social standing, and present the incomparable Healer who never overlooks the penitent's supplication.

Thirdly, Jesus also mingled with wealthy people.

Meanwhile, Jesus was in Bethany at the home of Simon, a man who had previously had leprosy. While he was eating, a woman came in with a beautiful alabaster jar of expensive perfume and poured it over his head (Matthew 26:6, 7, NLT).

There was a man named Nicodemus, a Jewish religious leader who was a Pharisee. After dark one evening, he came to speak with Jesus (John 3:1, 2, NLT).

He took his twelve disciples with him, along with some women who had been cured of evil spirits and diseases. Among them were Mary Magdalene, from whom he had cast out seven demons; Joanna, the wife of Chuza, Herod's business manager; Susanna; and many others who were contributing from their own resources to support Jesus and his disciples (Luke 8:1–3, NLT).

Jesus loves everybody, including wealthy people. Christ expressed that love by seeking their companionship. Dinners, private meetings, public gatherings, and other social situations formed the background of several memorable encounters with successful people. Such opportunities exist today. The following list will suggest occasions whereby readers can likewise mingle with wealthier people in contemporary settings.

1. Civic organizations. Many well-to-do people take their citizenship and civic responsibilities seriously. Such civic-minded persons frequently join service organizations such as Kiwanis International. Their prior orientation toward service may indicate spiritual awakening, personal humility, or other favorable characteristics. People with moderate wealth participate equally alongside their wealthier counterparts. Obviously, this creates multiple opportunities for interaction and possible friendship. While disparities of wealth may exist, many well-heeled individuals recognize that they share many commonalities with others. Everybody gets hungry. Everyone becomes weary sometime. Mingling with affluent associates normally reduces or eliminates social barriers.

2. School functions. In several countries, public education has blunted the social distinctions caused by discrepancies in wealth. Some school districts mandate school uniforms to downplay socioeconomic differences. Younger children especially seem oblivious to class divisions. These children select playmates based upon compatibility, similar interests, and other factors that exclude family wealth. School activities, therefore, provide a leveled playing field where children and their parents can build friendships. United through extracurricular activities and educational pursuits, families of various income levels can discover mutual interests and much common ground.

3. Business and professional associations. Abraham, Solomon, Joseph of Arimathea, and dozens more exemplify the class of wealthy believers. Such believers can extend their influence through participation in organizations formed to promote the common interests of its membership. When carefully and prayerfully selected, even political activism can fall into this category. While the organizing principle of these groups might be continuing education, taxation reform, or something else, the grouping of like-minded people offers many friendship-building opportunities.

4. Service positions. Naaman's servant certainly did not qualify as an equal, yet she effectively transformed his life through her witness. Many modern believers, who regularly serve wealthy patrons, may enjoy similar opportunities and results. Cooks, nannies, caddies, chauffeurs, housekeepers, receptionists, gardeners, repairpersons, mechanics, and countless others can witness by remembering their exalted heavenly standing, honing their spiritual recognition, and patiently waiting for divine opportunities. Social inequality is not necessarily an impediment to effective witnessing.

5. Leisure industries. Whereas poorer people cannot afford extensive vacations, luxury liner cruises, and overseas excursions, wealthy people habitually pursue leisure, often to demonstrate their elevated status. Superiority is established through taking the most enviable vacation. Leisure offers Christians unique avenues for witnessing that may disappear during office hours. Mental relaxation and physical recreation resonate well with themes of grace and release.

6. Health ministry. Illness forms the great equalizer. Heart disease claims prince and pauper alike. Cancer destroys wealthy tissue and indigent tissue. Accidents afflict universally without regard for socioeconomic standing. The only difference fortune makes in death is the extravagance of the coffin. Medical personnel, therefore, have unique openings to share spiritual truth with their wealthy patients. Facing death or substantial debilitation, even the arrogant sometimes become willing recipients of divine favor.

7. Specialized interest groups. This could include any group centered about a designated pursuit, often recreational in nature: radio-controlled airplane groups, golfing associations, bowling leagues, equestrian racing, symphonic guilds, choral societies, artists' fellowships, and so on. Because these groups are unified through common interests, rather than socioeconomic strata, the discrepancies between incomes are downplayed, facilitating friendships across socioeconomic divisions. Obviously, the activities listed above require some financial investment. The amounts, however, are often within reach for middle-class individuals and, when viewed from a missionary standpoint, represent a spiritual investment.

Discipleship

For generations Christians have demonstrated considerable sympathy for those from poorer classes. Feeding the hungry, sheltering the homeless, parenting the orphans, and lifting the masses through education, opportunity, and economic development have drawn widespread support. But where has passionate concern for the salvation of wealthy individuals gone? They thrive financially, but spiritually? Does their abundance of possessions blind us to their spiritual poverty? Have Christians forgotten that money cannot buy personal significance, spiritual purpose, and ultimate meaning? The poorest believers have what the wealthiest entrepreneurs desperately seek.

Therefore none should feel intimidated by riches because, as royal heirs, Christians possess much greater treasure than anything this world produces. Like Naaman's servant, they should stand ready to witness whenever and wherever God's Spirit opens hearts. Like cardiac specialists, they should train themselves to recognize spiritual heart conditions and be prepared to administer divine grace, the only proven cure for human brokenness. By mingling with prosperous people, establishing meaningful friendships, becoming sensitive to spiritual neediness, and always being prepared to communicate the gospel, modern Christians *will* lead the wealthy to Christ.

---

1.   Walter B. Knight, *Knight's Illustrations for Today* (Chicago: Moody Press, 1977), 274.

CHAPTER 9

The word *powerful* does not necessarily mean prosperous, but authority and wealth usually clasp hands tightly. Therefore the principles advanced in the previous chapter have some application here. Authority, however, originates from locations other than wealth—prominently from religion and politics or government. Understanding the nature of these entities may help us develop methodologies for reaching those entrusted with their leadership.

Religion

Common misunderstandings and superficial definitions have separated religion and spirituality in the contemporary mind-set. Youth, especially, opine, "I'm extremely spiritual but really hate religion." Ironically, religion and spirituality define our relationships with supernatural phenomena. Acknowledging the existence of supernatural dimensions can reveal humility. Something, someone, somehow lies beyond the realm of touching, seeing, hearing, and smelling. Science fiction and modernistic religions sometimes identify this power using terms such as *the Force,* but traditional religions ordinarily prefer *God.* However one understands the supernatural, the spiritual quest endeavors to unite human beings with something or Someone greater than themselves. Evil's existence is typically explained within this context. Personal or societal wickedness becomes the barrier to be surmounted so that contact with God can be achieved.

The importance of reaching God cannot be overestimated because, without this contact, personal wholeness cannot be realized. Religious formulations for attaining this wholeness differ slightly with each religion, but certain elements emerge repeatedly.

1. Punishment versus appeasement. Wickedness is destructive; therefore, wicked actions must be punished. Death should be the expected punishment unless God's anger can somehow be averted. Anciently petitioners offered animal sacrifices, thinking this would somehow satisfy divine requirements for righteousness. Fearful religionists participated in elaborate ceremonies in hopes of appeasing divine wrath. Variously, paganism, Islam, Buddhism, and certain expressions of Christianity established different systems that provided perceived escape routes. Within Christianity, financial contributions (indulgences) and ecclesiastical services eventually replaced animal sacrifices, while other religions incorporated self-flagellation and forms of psychological self-torture for settling accounts with God. When the processes for atonement (at-one-ment or union with God) became institutionalized, this gave the priesthood, the religious leadership, incomparable power. Eternal destinies and often social inclusion depended upon their decisions. Opposing them could signify eternal damnation and social isolation.

2. Experience and presence. Union with God involves spatial dimension, either literally or metaphorically. Stated otherwise, knowing God is about "location, location, location." Historically, Judaism placed monumental emphasis upon the temple sanctuary. This location was where humanity approached divinity, where common human beings met Jehovah. God's presence was anchored in Jerusalem, not in those hillside shrines, not in those substitute worship centers of Samaria, and certainly not in heathen temples. Physical remembrances were constructed at definite physical locations where God had been encountered. After the Israelites crossed Jordan, they assembled stones to commemorate the miracle. Jacob's encounter with the heavenly ladder was likewise commemorated with a pillar. The Samaritan woman challenged Jesus regarding the proper location for authentic worship. Christ's disciples excitedly clamored for a physical memorial following the heavenly encounter at the mount of transfiguration.

Experiencing God's presence was inextricably linked with specific physical locations. When access to these locations, and thus access to God, was controlled through an earthly priesthood, those priests possessed tremendous power. Jesus complained that these priests not only refused to embrace God themselves but that they also blockaded the passageway leading to God. When the restored blind man testified for Christ, his parents distanced themselves, fearing expulsion from the synagogue (John 9). Such power absolutely exceeded the influence that wealth alone afforded.

The divergence between religion and spirituality, as commonly conceived, seems rooted around the concept of control. Spirituality is understood as the individual's desire for spiritual union with God, whereas, religion is identified with people trying to control others' attempts to reach God. This identification of religion with outside control probably explains why first-century Israelites feared and resented their priesthood. They feared that crossing the religious leadership would compromise their hope for salvation, but they resented the hypocrisy exhibited by ministers who demanded something from their adherents that they failed to exemplify themselves. Actions spoke louder than words. Understanding how religion originates power helps us comprehend how Christ could both confront and convert these religious power brokers.

Government or politics

Whereas religious authority originates within our longing for divine union and apprehension of death, governmental authority is established on societal foundations. Biblically speaking, government has solid underpinnings.

> Let every person be subject to the governing authorities; for there is no authority except from God, and those authorities that exist have been instituted by God. Therefore whoever resists authority resists what God has appointed, and those who resist will incur judgment. For rulers are not a terror to good conduct, but to bad. Do you wish to have no fear of the authority? Then do what is good, and you will receive its approval; for it is God's servant for your good. But if you do what is wrong, you should be afraid, for the authority does not bear the sword in vain! It is the servant of God to execute wrath on the wrongdoer. Therefore one must be subject, not only because of wrath but also because of conscience (Romans 13:1–5, NRSV).

Societies, whether recognizing God's guidance or not, nevertheless establish guidelines, regulations, standards, and directives to govern social interaction and societal relationships. Marriage, business and commerce, basic human rights, privacy, personal freedoms, security, and countless other matters are subjects for negotiation within the context of government. Without government, anarchy would reign supreme and physical strength alone would determine morality. Stronger people would accomplish their wishes to the detriment of everyone else.

Countries where drug kingpins reign alongside elected governments illustrate this power principle. Sometimes cocaine manufacturers actually control the government because their arsenals are substantially larger than the government's. In strong democratic societies, money purchases advertising to persuade, whereas in autocratic systems, money purchases firepower to compel. The primary point is that government restrains this strongman mentality, which easily degenerates into "might equals right." Government, ideally at least, preserves cultures from chaotic interactions, providing order, stability, and confident optimism. Although earthly governments, including better ones, fall short of divine perfection, they are preferable to having none whatsoever.

The government's role has steadily increased. Roman caesars satisfied themselves with world conquest, facilitating commerce, and quelling rebellions—minor accomplishments by contemporary standards. Today's government, in some countries, assumes responsibility for nourishing, medicating, birthing, burying, and everything in between. Citing security reasons, citizens from traditionally democratic societies have willingly surrendered their constitutional rights purchased with the sacrifices of previous generations.

The notable difference between today's world and the ancient one is geographical. The Waldenses could escape to the mountaintops. Pilgrims found refuge within the American wilderness. Where does impenetrable wilderness exist today? Commercial buildings, recreational facilities, public libraries, government offices, and neighborhood convenience stores utilize surveillance technology. Governmental power has become pervasive.

Unfortunately, there is great truth in the aphorism "Absolute power corrupts absolutely." Powerful people can scarcely resist the temptation to deify themselves. Anciently, Roman caesars did this officially, assuming divine titles and prerogatives. Contemporary societies accomplish this surreptitiously. Rather than claiming God's titles outright, the leadership contents itself with assuming God's prerogatives. Presidents and prime ministers undertake the mission of determining right from wrong.

Chapter 9

Religionists give themselves the assignment of becoming salvation's gate-keepers. Other power brokers assume authority to determine economic and social matters. God's scriptural instructions are willfully ignored. Human musings are substituted instead and elevated to the highest positions.

When modern believers recognize the powerful allure of power, they can begin to appreciate the enormous difficulty of reaching powerful people. Christ found this group His most challenging. Pilate, Herod Antipas, Caiaphas, Annas, and perhaps several more ignored, ridiculed, and rejected Jesus. Felix, Festus, and Herod Agrippa (Herod Antipas's nephew) continued that tradition, bypassing Paul's gospel presentation. Still, there were conversions: Jairus, a religious leader (Mark 5), the unnamed Roman military officer (Luke 7), Nicodemus and Joseph of Arimathea (John 3; 19:38). The continuing ministry of Jesus' followers contributed other triumphs: "So God's message continued to spread. The number of believers greatly increased in Jerusalem, and many of the Jewish priests were converted, too" (Acts 6:7, NLT).

Saul, renamed Paul, abandoned a promising career in religious leadership to become Christ's disciple. Afterward, Paul, together with Barnabas, was instrumental in leading Sergius Paulus, the Cyprian governor, to Christianity. Philip the evangelist converted the Ethiopian treasurer, who served in Queen Candace's official cabinet. Cornelius, the Italian regimental captain, received salvation through Peter's ministry. Crispus, another synagogue leader, was likewise converted through Timothy and Paul's witnessing.

What circumstances attended these conversions? What lessons can modern believers derive from these narratives that will inform their efforts to effectively convey the gospel message during the twenty-first century?

Lesson 1: Boldness

"You will stand trial before governors and kings because you are my followers. But this will be your opportunity to tell the rulers and other unbelievers about me. When you are arrested, don't worry about how to respond or what to say. God will give you the right words at the right time. For it is not you who will be speaking—it will be the Spirit of your Father speaking through you" (Matthew 10:18–20, NLT).

"Don't worry in advance about how to answer the charges against you, for I will give you the right words and such wisdom that none of your opponents will be able to reply or refute you" (Luke 21:14, 15, NLT).

"You will receive power when the Holy Spirit comes upon you. And you will be my witnesses, telling people about me everywhere—in Jerusalem, throughout Judea, in Samaria, and to the ends of the earth" (Acts 1:8, NLT).

Jesus encouraged radical boldness. Confronting governors, emperors, plus other leaders was not merely possible but expected. Divine wisdom, irrefutable presentations, divinely chosen vocabulary, and miraculous power would attend those faithful believers who fearlessly communicated the gospel message to powerful leaders.

Oftentimes believers excuse themselves from God's commission. Moses' response was, "Send Aaron!" "Moses protested to God, 'Who am I to appear before Pharoah?' " (Exodus 3:11, NLT). Separated from God's grace and our divine calling, we are nothing. Under divine commission, however, believers become transformed into royal ambassadors, advancing kingdom objectives, fearlessly proclaiming heavenly realities. Moses' question was faithless. This was cowardice not humility. How many contemporary Christians imitate Moses today. "I'm unequivocally insignificant—a doormat-variety nobody. I'm timid, socially awkward, totally lacking self-confidence, intimidated by powerful people, and practically afraid of my shadow. Please send Aaron."

Does God validate such inexplicable excuses? Never. The often-repeated aphorism still rings true today: "God doesn't call the qualified; He qualifies the called." Has God appointed you to represent Him before senators, assemblypersons, presidents, prime ministers, and corporation superstars? Why hesitate? God's calling equals divine enabling. Most likely the person intimidating you will die within seventy-five years. You are scheduled for eternity.

My first regular employment was with Naval Air Station, Pensacola, Florida. Most civilian bosses there were former military and proved it with incessant commands and orders. Before accepting employment, I had spelled out certain principles that I would not violate under any circumstances. The employer hired me anyway. Nevertheless, shortly thereafter, the employer demanded that I violate those principles. When I refused, threats followed. Fearful, yet ironically undaunted, I refused to compromise. I was not terminated, nor was I penalized with reduced hours or decreased remuneration, and my Christian principles were honored thereafter.

Lesson 2: Patience

Christ's nighttime encounter with Nicodemus did *not* cause an immediate conversion (John 3). A seed was nonetheless implanted. Years afterward, that seed flourished, taking root and bearing fruit. Some believers apparently become discouraged whenever instantaneous conversions fail to happen.

Remember three things: First, conversion does *not* depend upon your eloquence or intelligence. Your abilities are not being evaluated. Conversion is God's responsibility and those who unwittingly usurp that divine prerogative are destined for disappointment. Better track coaches demand their athletes' best efforts; however, they do not demand that they win. Likewise, our heavenly Father expects His believers' best efforts. When contemplating eternal realities, life-and-death decisions, and the possibility of everlasting extinction, how can believers do anything less? God, however, never placed the responsibility for converting people in human hands. Soul winning is forever the Holy Spirit's province.

Second, even Jesus lost Judas. His inner circle mutinied. Jesus witnessed to Caiaphas, Pontius Pilate, Herod Antipas, Annas, and probably many other leaders whose stories are not recorded in Scripture. Apparently, none of these leaders was converted. Does that excuse modern believers from witnessing before royal households and politically powerful people? Obviously not! Nevertheless, high expectations must be tempered with realistic hopes. We may not win everyone but if we generate lackluster, halfhearted efforts we will certainly reach none.

Third, persistence is the twin of patience. Patience indicates endurance, the characteristic of remaining hopeful rather than becoming exasperated, the ability to travel toward stated objectives when obstructions present themselves. Persistence constitutes the action verb for patience. Patience means knowing you will finish the marathon although your body presently screams that you cannot proceed farther. Persistence means multiplying step after step after step until crossing the finish line. Patience is heart; persistence is muscle. What persistent actions are you taking whenever your initial attempts to reach powerful people are callously or carelessly rebuffed? Are your efforts fading during the first mile of the 26.2-mile marathon? Are your endeavors dwindling around the twenty-fifth? The question regards effort rather than outcomes; determination rather than results; not if you won but if you finished.

We probably should expect from the outset that it will take longer for powerful people to reach life-changing decisions. Luke records, "Agrippa interrupted him. 'Do you think you can persuade me to become a Christian so quickly?' " (Acts 26:28, NLT). Nebuchadnezzar's humiliation lasted seven years before he acknowledged God's sovereignty. Many priests heard Jesus' message, witnessed His miracles, and longed to follow Him. Years passed, however, before Luke recorded, "So God's message continued to spread. The number of believers greatly increased in Jerusalem, and many of the Jewish priests were converted, too" (Acts 6:7, NLT). Social entanglements, political obligations, and financial considerations may contribute to their carelessness (John 12:41–43). Nevertheless, we should never lose hope, always exercising patience through unfailing prayer.

Lesson 3: Timeliness

Hubris occurs whenever God's well-intentioned people presumptuously proceed ahead of His leading. Negligence occurs whenever God's indolent people fall behind. The safest course remains staying in step alongside God's moving. How should believers discern whether they are ahead or behind? Prayer and earnest systematic Bible study form the foundation of effective communication with God. Without effective communication, we could be deceived.

During the Second World War, the Allied forces deciphered the encryptions that concealed their enemies' communications. Furnished with this inside information, they learned when they should attack, where vulnerable fortifications could be breached, what their troop strength was, and so forth. The enemy's diversionary tactics were ineffective because the Allied forces could distinguish between deceptive activity and genuine troop movements. This provided an unbeatable advantage and doubtless shortened the conflict.

Daily prayer and regular Bible study are necessary preconditions for hearing God's directives. Running ahead may unnecessarily offend lost souls, while running behind may lose them altogether. One Christian couple approached their pastor, excited that their neighbors were displaying a strong spiritual interest. The minister encouraged them to exploit this spiritual opening through Bible studies. The couple deferred, thinking this was premature. The neighbors' spiritual vacuum went unfilled, and within three weeks, representatives of some religious cult had started studying with them, thus destroying their interest in the authentic gospel. Had the Christian couple synchronized with Heaven's timing a different story might be written.

Among powerful people some occasions may signal an increased responsiveness or receptivity. These generally share one common thread: *power failure* or *a loss of control*. Pride about controlling life's events generates false security. Whenever control wavers, this false security is threatened. During these vulnerable periods, people sometimes escape their imprisonment within self-confidence. They investigate options outside themselves, including Jesus Christ.

These occasions may include the following:

1. Debilitating illness. Nebuchadnezzar suffered with clinical lycanthropy. Hezekiah's disease had spiritual implications. Naaman's sickness stimulated his search for answers. Drug addiction would be included in this category.

2. Bereavement. Jairus, the esteemed synagogue leader, might never have encountered Jesus except for his daughter's illness and subsequent death.

3. Divorce. Nothing undercuts personal self-esteem more deeply than a disintegrating family. Failure in this arena destroys the appearance of stability. It questions the person's ability to maintain relationships and function effectively.

4. Unemployment. This especially pertains to gentlemen. Male egoism centers about values derived through their vocation. Whenever employment is threatened the male self-identity is terrorized. Charles Colson's loss of position and subsequent prosecution and incarceration, in the Watergate scandal of the 1970s, eventually steered him toward authentic Christianity.

5. Personal emptiness. This is more difficult to discern because no particular event necessarily signals its presence. Some would equate this with midlife crisis. Age does not necessarily determine this factor but oftentimes younger people are blinded with life's pursuits until one morning they awaken and realize their accumulations, collections, and achievements are meaningless. Solomon's literary masterpiece, Ecclesiastes, details his realization that without God's blessing every achievement becomes ultimately worthless. Sometimes power brokers also reach this realization.

Lesson 4: Readiness

Everything else previously discussed becomes useless when readiness is lacking. How many believers have attended witnessing workshops, soul-winning seminars, and discipleship rallies who have never shared their personal testimony, opened the Bible to unbelievers, or even prayed with another person regarding his or her salvation? Imagine the consequences of having absentee soldiers. Millions of dollars in training expense, coupled with hours of backbreaking effort, would be sacrificed if soldiers failed to perform their assigned duties. Instead, soldiers live on constant alert, looking for opportunities to exercise their training.

Ananias was one reticent but obedient soldier. Saul's Damascus mission was to persecute Christ's followers. Jesus interrupted that mission with blinding light, rendering Saul absolutely helpless. Someone had to present Saul with the gospel message and God selected Ananias for that assignment. Imagine being awakened midsleep and receiving heavenly instructions to evangelize the most notorious murderer of Christians known at that time! You probably would schedule an appointment with your hearing specialist immediately. Although questioning his sanity, Ananias clearly recognized his Master's voice and obediently fulfilled his assignment. Scripture records,

> Ananias went and entered the house. He laid his hands on Saul and said, "Brother Saul, the Lord Jesus, who appeared to you on your way here, has sent me so that you may regain your sight and be filled with the Holy Spirit" (Acts 9:17, NRSV).

This otherwise anonymous disciple was prepared to accomplish God's mission although trepidation attended his steps. What marvelous results. Ananias's one known disciple became the foremost Christian missionary to the Mediterranean world, the author of fourteen biblical epistles, and a faithful martyr. Millions of conversions may indirectly be attributed to Ananias's faithful labor.

What emerging history-changing evangelist might God be calling you to reach today? Your college professor? Your senator? Your government minister? Like Ananias, you can stand ready to answer God's calling.

By understanding what motivates powerful people to pursue power, by becoming sensitive to the spiritual needs of this class, by allowing God to schedule our witness, and by standing ready always to accept His assignments, Christians will witness effectively to politicians, religious leaders, judges, and other authorities. God is still in control!

CHAPTER 10

Charles Chang migrated to the United States, ostensibly to pursue advanced piano keyboard instruction. Already considered prodigious, this teenager leveraged his impressive skills to warrant the elusive American study visa. Charles genuinely wanted opportunities to improve his keyboard proficiency and qualified instructors were located around universities—Christian universities. However, his inquiry involved substantially more than was immediately apparent. Christian universities were researched because this youngster deeply desired Christian instruction and baptism, that is, conversion, which was forbidden by the atheistic communist regime that governed his country.

Charles's host family arranged Christian mentorship. Weekly Bible studies fanned the spiritual flames within his heart. Ironically, Charles's mentor could not speak his language and Charles was not proficient with English. However, he possessed a bilingual Bible written in English and his language. Charles's mentor simply directed him to pertinent biblical passages that he could comprehend in his native language. Following months of investigation into Christianity, this talented teenager affirmed his acceptance of Christ as his personal Savior and was baptized. Shortly thereafter, he moved to study with another pianist before returning to his homeland.

The believers who witnessed Charles's baptism were treated to a similar experience sometime later. Sabrina Chung's son had immigrated to the United States where he taught engineering. His spiritual journey crossed paths with numerous Christians. Finding his national atheism meaningless and unfulfilling, he studied Christianity, encountered Christ personally, and surrendered his life to Jesus. Sabrina was intrigued with her son's newfound allegiance. Although elderly, she began exploring this foreign faith. Exploration evolved into conviction and eventually flowered into conversion. While she was visiting with her transplanted American family, her son arranged Bible studies with his mentor. The circumstances were strangely similar—Sabrina understood little English while her mentor's comprehension of her language was negligible. Sometimes utilizing her son's interpretive abilities and sometimes depending upon bilingual translations, she learned the fundamental doctrines of Christianity. Before returning to her native country, she was likewise baptized.

Who would have dreamed that an American congregation would be privileged to send two native missionaries into an atheistic communist territory. What geographical boundaries, what national frontiers, what cultural differences could separate them from God's love?

> My house shall be called a house of prayer for all peoples (Isaiah 56:7, MLB).

> Gentiles shall come to your light, and kings to the brightness of your rising (Isaiah 60:3, *Lamsa*).

> Some Greeks were among those who came to worship during the Passover festival. They went to Philip (who was from Bethsaida in Galilee) and told him, "Sir, we would like to meet Jesus" (John 12:20, 21, GOD'S WORD).

> Gentiles are not foreigners or strangers any longer; you are now citizens together with God's people and members of the family of God. You, too, are built upon the foundation laid by the apostles and prophets, the cornerstone being Christ Jesus himself (Ephesians 2:19, 20, TEV).

> They were amazed and in their astonishment exclaimed, "Why, they are all Galileans, are they not, these men who are speaking? How is it then that we hear them, each of us in his own native

language? Parthians, Medes, Elamites; inhabitants of Mesopotamia, of Judaea and Cappadocia, of Pontus and Asia, of Phrygia and Pamphylia, of Egypt and the district of Libya around Cyrene; visitors from Rome, both Jews and proselytes, Cretans and Arabs, we hear them telling in our own tongues the great things God has done" (Acts 2:7–11, NEB).

"Make disciples of all nations, baptizing them in the name of the Father and of the Son and of the Holy Spirit, teaching them to observe all that I have commanded you" (Matthew 28:19, 20, ESV).

"When I am lifted up from the earth, I shall draw all men to myself" (John 12:32, *Jerusalem Bible*).

These passages represent the iceberg's tip when considering the universal, global, Christian message. This message cannot be confined, contained, nor inhibited. People everywhere have the inalienable right to hear about Jesus. No nationality monopolizes Christ.

Understanding the concept of the *universal Savior* is foundational to authentic Christian ministry. Jesus loves everyone. Zealous teachers, overanxious for promoting the personal relationship with God, have encouraged believers to individualize John 3:16. How often have speakers for youth conferences admonished their listeners to personalize this passage by substituting their personal name for "the world"? Although it is well intentioned, this approach can foster self-centeredness. Narcissistic believers start feeling entitled, privileged, superior, and, perhaps, arrogant. Pharisees and disciples alike suffered from this spiritual misunderstanding. Both seriously questioned the possibility that other nationalities could experience salvation. Jesus demonstrated that anyone of faith could experience His kingdom's blessings.

A woman whose little daughter had an unclean spirit immediately heard about him, and she came and bowed down at his feet. Now the woman was a Gentile, of Syrophoenician origin. She begged him to cast the demon out of her daughter. He said to her, "Let the children be fed first, for it is not fair to take the children's food and throw it to the dogs." But she answered him,

"Sir, even the dogs under the table eat the children's crumbs."
Then he said to her, "For saying that, you may go—the demon
has left your daughter" (Mark 7:25–29, NRSV).

While Jesus maintained that His primary mission was "feeding" Israel, this desperate mother's extreme faith provided the opportunity for
Christ to broaden that mission. Consistent with ancient prophetic tradition (Isaiah 19:19–25; 66:18–21; Micah 4:1–4; Zechariah 8:20–23) Jesus
flings open heaven's storehouse, honoring this Syrophoenician's uncompromising reliance upon Himself.

The universality of the gospel predicted anciently through prophecy
glimmers expectantly throughout this poignant story. Jesus becomes the
Messiah, not for Israel alone, but for every earthly inhabitant. Christ
likewise healed Samaritan lepers (Luke 17:11–19), received Greek visitors
during Passover (John 12; Josephus, in his history, mentions foreigners
worshiping at Jerusalem during Passover), and championed the good Samaritan (Luke 10:27–37).

Ironically, Christ's Jewish opponents unwittingly anticipated Jesus'
broader inclusive mission. During one Festival of Tabernacles, Jesus was
accosted by temple police. When Jesus announced that shortly they
would not find Him, they ridiculed him, saying, "Where does this man
intend to go that we will not find him? Does he intend to go to the Dis-
persion among the Greeks and teach the Greeks?" (John 7:35, NRSV).
Their thinking was, *What could be more demeaning?*

Another ironic twist surfaces in Caiaphas's statement regarding
Christ's upcoming crucifixion. "Being high priest that year he prophesied that Jesus was about to die for the [Jewish] nation, and *not for the
nation only,* but to gather into one the dispersed children of God" (John
11:51, 52, NRSV; emphasis added). Jesus' disciples, especially Paul,
spearheaded that spiritual juggernaut. Christ reassured Ananias, saying,
"Saul [renamed Paul] is my chosen instrument to take my message to the
Gentiles" (Acts 9:15, NLT). Alongside Paul was Barnabas, Silas, Christ's
original disciples, and countless others who labored tirelessly to fulfill
Jesus' prediction: "This Good News of the Kingdom shall be proclaimed
throughout the whole world to set the evidence before all the Gentiles"
(Matthew 24:14, WNT). John's Apocalypse also trumpeted, "I saw another angel flying in mid-heaven, holding the everlasting Gospel to proclaim to the inhabitants of the earth—to every nation and tribe and

language and people" (Revelation 14:6, Phillips).

The book of Acts still serves Christians everywhere as the primary textbook for cross-cultural evangelism—evangelizing people groups beyond your own. Paul's missionary journeys are recorded there. Peter's vision regarding cultural barriers is recorded there. Philip's evangelization of the Ethiopian eunuch is likewise included. Practical matters regarding worship and social interaction among culturally different peoples are modeled through the Jerusalem council's deliberations. The template for effective boundary-jumping soul winning is contained within these pages. Strategies and methodologies may be extrapolated from the narratives. Inspiration and encouragement is likewise discovered there. What, specifically, can believers gather from Acts?

The book of Acts constitutes Luke's second history. His first, the Gospel narrative, recounts Christ's earthly activity from birth until death. Luke apparently believed, however, that this was insufficient. Knowing Christ's personal history and sacrifice was primary, but knowing their subsequent effect upon actual people was crucial. What difference did Christ's ransom make for the day-to-day choices of everyday people during His physical absence? Thus, Luke's second manuscript provided the answer to that question. God's Spirit first transformed their lives, then ignited the inconsumable passion that agitated the civilized world. The foremost lesson from Luke's second volume is that God occupies the position of Executive Director.

The first personnel decision of the Christian church was finding Judas's replacement. While humans nominated candidates for this position, the final choosing was determined by God Himself (Acts 1:23–26). The Communications Director (foreign-language division) was the Holy Spirit (Acts 2). He likewise served as Speech Instructor (Acts 4:8; 7), Transportation Director (Acts 8:26–40), principal Recruitment Officer (Acts 9:15; 13:2; 20:28), Conflict-Resolution Specialist (Acts 15, especially verse 28), Financial Fraud Investigator (Acts 5), Prison-Ministries Coordinator (Acts 4; 16; 21–28), Master Strategist (Acts 16:6–10; 20:22–24), Publications Administrator (Acts 28:25; 2 Peter 1:19–21), Medical Director (Acts 9:17–19), Equal Salvation Opportunity Commissioner (Acts 10:30–36; 11:18), and Educational Superintendent (Acts 1:8; 4:31; 13:4–9; John 16:12–15). Without God's Divine Spirit, there is no mission!

Another valuable insight springs from those pages that record Peter's vision. Peter declares, "I truly understand that God shows no partiality [favoritism], but in every nation anyone who fears him and does what is right is acceptable to him" (Acts 10:34, 35, NRSV). God must be the acknowledged Chief Executive and His attitude toward other peoples must prevail. Christian siblinghood constitutes biblical equality. Peter's rationale for including Gentiles within God's family was simple: because Gentiles received the Holy Spirit's outpouring, Jews cannot withhold inclusion within God's family (Acts 10:44–11:18). Substantial numbers of Jews agreed with that intellectually, yet were unprepared to handle it emotionally. Culturally speaking, they could accept these Gentiles should they willingly adopt Jewish customs, most notably, circumcision.

Similar temptations prove to be fatal attractions for contemporary Christians. Western missionaries, particularly, have been accused of coupling westernization or Americanization with Christian disciple-making. Question: Can people become Christians without becoming westernized? Has God commissioned believers to announce Christ's atoning sacrifice or promote American cultural standards? No doubt, some reader is thinking that cultural equality is being promoted herein. Absolutely not!

Obviously, some cultures reflect Christian principles more closely than others. Who would knowingly exchange democratic civilization for a cannibalistic society? Nevertheless, extreme caution should be exercised to ensure that Christian principles, rather than nationalistic customs, are taught. Requiring something of believers that Christ has not required violates one cardinal principle of Christianity—liberty. Because eastern, western, southern, and northern believers have equally received God's outpouring, making them essentially equal, they can learn from each other, rather than one group dominating the others. Wherever cultures genuinely have better ideas in some areas than others, these are more effectively advanced through recommendation rather than imperial mandate.

Another timeless principle contained in Acts is flexibility. Humility, open-mindedness, and creativity should be considered related and supportive concepts. Paul's strategic plan anticipated preaching throughout Asia (the province, not the continent). Jesus' Spirit blockaded that scheme. Subsequently, Paul headed north toward Bithynia. Once again the Holy Spirit obstructed Paul's advance. Finally, God revealed *His* strategy: evangelize Macedonia. Suddenly, barricades disappeared as Paul discerned and implemented God's design. Because Paul remained flexible, willing to follow God's leading rather than willfully prosecuting his predetermined strategy, God greatly empowered him. Paul's flexibility demonstrated humility. Although he certainly had ideas about how to execute his preaching assignment, he was nonetheless pliable, willingly shaped by the Holy Spirit's foresight.

Oftentimes believers stubbornly pursue their cherished opinions about promoting God's work despite prevailing counsel from other believers that points in a different direction. Other believers, however, are open-minded. They recognize their personal limitations, finding others' contributions and opinions to be valuable. Open-mindedness usually courts creativity. Frequently, narrow-minded people see things only one way. Lacking creativity, they cannot fathom alternative pathways. Contrarily, creative people derive pleasure from finding multiple means of accomplishing given objectives. When one plan collapses, they develop another one. Failure does not bring discouragement. Failure eliminates nonviable options and oftentimes provides the knowledge that brings about success. Noncreative people suffer from a limited vision, while creative people perceive limitless possibilities. Somehow creativity facilitates flexibility.

Dependence upon the Holy Spirit, recognition of human equality, and personal flexibility have been hallmarks of successful cross-cultural evangelism from the first century until the twenty-first. Obviously, other general principles discussed throughout earlier chapters—biblical centrality, fervent intercessory prayer, creative instruction, and personal sacrifice—are likewise important.

Investigate the exploits of William Carey, Adoniram Judson, Hudson Taylor, Amy Carmichael, Gladys Aylward, David Livingstone, and hundreds more who introduced the gospel message across geographical and cultural boundaries. These characteristics surface repeatedly. Motivated by disinterested benevolence and a divine compulsion to redeem lost humanity, they identified themselves—through fashion, eating habits, language, cultural traditions, and social conventions—with those they sought to evangelize. They mingled freely, participating with their newfound friends at their workplaces, their leisure hangouts, and their humble dwellings. Through their cultural immersion and Christian witness, they secured their confidence. When they presented Christ, verbally and nonverbally, people were drawn by their friendship, character, and lifestyle. Those stories must be repeated today.

Are we saying that everyone should leave their jobs, purchase tickets for unknown destinations, and abandon everything to advance God's kingdom and fulfill the Great Commission? Not necessarily. Remember, God's Spirit serves as Chief Personnel Officer. Divine appointment *alone* qualifies the believer for cross-cultural service. How many mission boards have discouraged God's chosen missionaries based solely upon human criteria? How many committees have blundered needlessly, turning away older believers, single females, and physically impaired persons?

Similarly, Samuel judged based upon outward appearance. Certainly David's older brothers—experienced fighting men, well built, handsome—were better suited for kingship. Fortunately, Samuel's lifetime practice of Spirit dependency prevailed. David—youthful, impetuous, and inexperienced—possessed the qualities God needed most. God designated David for his service and Samuel anointed him king.

Several people who were spurned by committees followed God's leading anyway. They planted churches, opened closed countries, translated Scripture, spearheaded Christian outreach, and fortunately recorded their stories.

How can Christians certainly know that they have been called to foreign ministry?

1. Deep-seated conviction. Leaving family and transplanting oneself, even considering the convenience of global aviation, should never be taken lightly. God beckons most Christians to be lights in their neighborhoods and hometowns. That fact notwithstanding, some believers receive a heavenly summons to traverse geographical and cultural boundaries to transplant the gospel. This will not be rooted in passing notions or fickle feelings. Believers thus summoned experience an *inescapable* conviction that cannot be easily shaken. Such people cannot be discouraged by human obstructions and cannot be dissuaded from accepting God's invitation.

The Old Testament records a narrative concerning a southern prophet who was commissioned to deliver God's message to the northern kingdom (1 Kings 13). God's incontrovertible instructions were to deliver the message and return immediately across the border. After completing his mission, he was returning home when another person, claiming the prophetic gift, stopped him, inviting him to delay his return. The unnamed southern prophet protested that his instructions forbade such delay. The other person claimed that God had given him a different message that granted permission for postponing his return. Rather than heeding God's clear instructions, the prophet accepted the lying prophet's declaration and stopped for dinner. Later resuming his journey he was savagely attacked and killed by lions—God's punishment for disobedience. Whenever God has implanted that inescapable conviction that one has been destined for cross-cultural ministry, that passion *must* be followed.

Cautions are appropriate here. Sometimes social misfits call themselves to foreign ministry because it accomplishes two things: first, it provides an escape from hurtful situations; and second, sometimes it generates positive attention. Escaping our inadequacies is definitely not the proper motivation for overseas ministry. The enticement of adventure sometimes attracts people to cross-cultural ministry. Seeing the world for Jesus has justified many "self-called" missionaries. This, however, does not constitute God's divine calling. Typically, those genuinely called initially struggle with the divine invitation. Like young Samuel, they wonder if their calling is merely of human origin. Then some modern Eli assures them that they are hearing God's voice. Heeding that voice they establish a lifetime connection through which they repeatedly discern God's leading.

2. Synchronized external support. Should circumstances providentially come together, this may supply some external evidence that supports the inward conviction. This might include (a) finding a life partner who shares comparable convictions regarding foreign ministry, (b) financial circumstances (houses selling immediately, strangers mysteriously providing financial support, etc.), or (c) unexplainable openings (lessened governmental opposition in receiving countries, expeditious approval of visas and other travel documents, family opposition miraculously turned around to support, etc.). Inescapable conviction matched with providential circumstances often forms overwhelming evidence that God has called one to cross-cultural ministry.

Does this mean that those whom God has not called overseas are excused from cross-cultural evangelism? Absolutely not! Globalization has indeed shrunk our planet. Americans settle credit card disputes with customer service representatives from India. International travel is epidemic. Monetary fluctuations occurring abroad threaten domestic retirement accounts. The Internet has established a global culture. Complete cultural isolation has become almost impossible. This international climate affords several opportunities to evangelistically minded believers.

Discipleship

The following suggestions are not exhaustive:

1. Domestic educational opportunities. Foreign exchange students have been matriculating at major universities for years. Is your congregation located near these educational institutions? Does your ministry enjoy a campus presence? Have you explored networking opportunities that engage international students? Their very presence indicates openness, a thirsting after knowledge, a predisposition favoring change. Their dislocation, although temporary, creates a friendship vacuum that your acquaintance could fill. Simple gestures—shared meals, social invitations, possibly inclusion in professional associations—may initiate relationships that culminate in spiritual conversations.

Wherever conversions happen, God's kingdom is doubly blessed. First, heaven rejoices whenever lost souls discover their origin, significance, and purpose. Second, returning to their native countries, these international students can naturally translate their authentic Christian lifestyle into culturally understandable forms. Foreign missionaries strive diligently over long periods to achieve an entry-level understanding of unfamiliar cultures and languages, whereas these international students already possess that knowledge. Establishing campus ministries focused on international students may become your contribution to accelerating the expansion of the gospel worldwide.

2. Media ministry. While radio, print, and television remain major players, the Internet has transformed the process of international communication. Multilingual people, especially, have virtually unlimited opportunities for transforming thought and creating the climate for conversion. International media ministry may simply mean sponsoring print subscriptions for people speaking other languages. Bloggers may initiate cross-cultural discussions regarding spirituality from any location, including their bedrooms. Equipment for producing quality radio and television programming has become more affordable for larger churches and smaller well-financed congregations. Christians are banding together in metropolitan areas and developing their own radio and television stations, even networks. Such electronic transmissions have penetrated iron curtains, bamboo curtains, and every other possible curtain. Such opportunities will not necessarily involve moving into unfamiliar countries and may be leveraged from wherever you live.

3. Short-term missions. Christian schools and church groups are increasingly participating in mission trips lasting from several days to several weeks. This system offers God's kingdom a twofold advantage. First, believers venture outside their comfort zones to experience life as others live it. Believers from wealthier nations encounter poverty first-hand. Oftentimes, especially among youth, this creates long-lasting impressions and sometimes establishes lifelong stewardship patterns. Experiencing this bigger picture makes Christians less inclined toward trivial church disputes back home because they are preoccupied with things that really matter. How many Christians return from such excursions and skirmish with fellow believers the following week about church bathroom decorations? They are more likely pondering strategies for feeding, sheltering, and educating the peasant farmers whom they worked alongside last week.

Second, many permanent contributions to kingdom growth have occurred through these short-term projects. Schools and church buildings have been erected. Houses have been rebuilt following natural disasters, creating inestimable positive feelings toward the indigenous and visiting believers. Sometimes curiosity regarding "foreign" speakers has drawn throngs to public evangelistic crusades resulting in hundreds, even thousands, of conversions.

4. Financial support. In westernized countries, challenging economic conditions have convinced many believers to curtail missions giving as concern for maintaining personal living standards increases. Christians thus minded are essentially saying, "Planet Earth is home." Investing in kingdom advancement has become secondary. Whereas simple lifestyle changes such as eating out less, utilizing more efficient automobiles, and restraining our unbridled materialism would free billions for cross-cultural evangelism, wealthy-nation Christians have become self-centered and self-serving.

Many believers, however, are honoring God by supporting world missions through sacrificial giving, rejoicing as God's promise to deliver immeasurable blessings is realized in their experience.

CHAPTER 11

Christ's foreknowledge of history, gathered through prophetic interpretation, indicated that His earthly sojourn would not be prolonged. Daniel's prophecies signaled a definite transitional point where His earthly ministry would terminate and heavenly ministry resume. Christ's fledgling church would be entrusted to the administration of willful, impetuous, and often contentious disciples following His departure. Bachelor's degrees generally require four years of concentrated university study. With barely *three* years at His disposal, Jesus sought to equip His disciples for spiritual leadership. The effectiveness of this training enterprise would largely determine the ongoing efficacy of their ministry and the survival of Christ's church. Only exceptional educational methodologies, premium training exercises, and time-tested practices would be employed.

Selective recruitment

Effective team building begins with effective recruitment. Effective recruitment begins with prayer (Acts 1:15–26). Divine wisdom must guide every step. Christ's parables suggest that everybody is not equally equipped. Some received five, others two, still others, one talent. Three disciples formed Christ's inner circle, giving them access to facets of Jesus' ministry not available to other followers. Twelve disciples formed another, broader, inner circle. Another group consisted of seventy-two individuals. Christ aligned them according to abilities given them by

God's sovereign design. None were required to perform better than their God-given capabilities allowed. Five-talent servants doubled their investment, but two-talent servants were not expected to produce ten. They were equally valued for doubling their investment to four. Placing two-talent people with five-talent responsibilities is equally unfair to the individuals and God's kingdom. The individuals become frustrated while the kingdom gets shortchanged. Conversely, placing five-talent people with two-talent responsibilities is irresponsible. The individuals become unchallenged (bored), while the kingdom gets shortchanged. Therefore, effective spiritual training begins with proper placement—matching the abilities, talents, dedication, and skills possessed by specific individuals with positions whereby they can flourish and effectively edify God's kingdom.

Obviously, matching individuals with specific responsibilities presupposes that the recruiter possesses thorough knowledge regarding a person's abilities and talents. Generally speaking, churches fail miserably here. Regional judicatories fare even worse. Possibly, this failure proceeds from a deathly misunderstanding of the church's essential nature and the pastoral role. Typically, pastors arrive with church plans rehashed from seminary lectures and their sermonic scheduled established. How many ministers arrive, thinking, *The pastor's primary role is empowering spiritual leadership to accomplish kingdom objectives and spiritual commissions. Therefore, my first year's primary occupation will be thoroughly acquainting myself with the Holy Spirit's gifting of our membership and matching them with responsibilities that enable them to spiritually flourish*?

Carrying out this process might yield that twelve-person inner circle, selecting those whose capabilities matched closest with the essential demands within that church's ministry. In medium- to larger-sized churches, pastors might prepare a select threesome gifted with discernment, hospitality, and spirituality to assist with this process of matching members with appropriate service opportunities and ministry responsibilities.

Regional judicatories should likewise thoroughly understand the unique endowments possessed by their ministers and the personalities of their congregations. Mismatching ministers with congregations predetermines failure. This cannot be effectively accomplished by making some cursory employment reference calls. That method works whenever the job description entails flipping burgers and cleaning tables but definitely fails whenever the job description involves leadership. This *requires* face-to-face, one-on-one contact.

Discipleship

Imagine Jesus writing the Galilean Fishermen's Association to reference Peter's work ethic and integrity, or the Internal Revenue Service to reference Matthew's accounting procedures. Christ engaged His disciples personally, directly, and congenially. Personal observation outdoes grapevine information.

How did Jesus transform these raw recruits into effective spiritual leaders?

Personal touches

Conventional contemporary education centers about classrooms. The classical definition of university lectures is, "The process whereby information is transferred from the professor's notebook to the student's without it passing through the mind of either." Does the transfer of information—even voluminous information—define education? Would imparting knowledge provide an adequate foundation for administering the worldwide gospel? Could typical classroom formatting convey wisdom, judgment, vision, discernment, humility, courage, patience, self-denial, philanthropy, compassion, and diplomacy?

Christ thought otherwise. Through shared experiences—living together, eating together, walking together, fishing together, and praying together—Jesus *modeled* spiritual leadership for His disciples. They watched Him confront religious ignorance and prejudice (Matthew 12:1–8), derived religious lessons from His impromptu mass caterings (Matthew 14:13–21), witnessed Him praying firsthand (Luke 5:16), personally encountered His otherworldly majesty (Matthew 17), and observed multiple healings (Mark 1:21–45). What lecture series could replace that involvement? Dusty streets, modest houses, scenic lakesides, temple courtyards, golden barley fields, aromatic vineyards—everywhere Jesus traveled—became their classroom. Jesus reached into their world, touching and transforming. Jesus changed His disciples' thinking without syllabi, textbooks, or virtual reality.

Sanctified knowledge

These wonderful experiences, however glorious, could never replace intelligent scriptural discovery. Biblical information, alone insufficient for spiritual transformation, was nevertheless a necessary component of Christ's leadership training. Through sermons and personal instruction, Jesus emphasized Scripture.

Scripture supplies an independent standard through which experiences may be measured. Moses forewarned Israel against the dangers involved with trusting personal experiences more than it did spiritual truth (Deuteronomy 13:1–5). Similarly, Isaiah upheld scriptural teaching and testimony as standards by which experiences might be judged (Isaiah 8:17–20). Christ's ministry aligned perfectly with Isaiah's clarion call: "Bind up the testimony; seal the teaching among my disciples" (verse 16, ESV). Unquestionably, the Holy Spirit's influence activates biblical teaching. Without this inspiration, biblical information is merely sentences, phrases, and thoughts. Coupled together, however, information and inspiration combine into an irrepressible revolutionary spiritual power to change hearts.

> "Don't misunderstand why I have come. I did not come to abolish the law of Moses or the writings of the prophets. No, I came to accomplish their purpose. I tell you the truth, until heaven and earth disappear, not even the smallest detail of God's law will disappear until its purpose is achieved" (Matthew 5:17, 18, NLT).

Closet rendezvous

Modern societies are preoccupied with "coming out of the closet." Jesus worried His disciples might never enter: "When thou prayest, enter into thy closet" (Matthew 6:6, KJV). We cannot speak often enough about prayer. Jesus' disciples must have sensed their need for prayer because they specifically asked Christ to teach them the manner of praying. Jesus' instruction focused on reverence, expectancy, surrender, dependence, confession and forgiveness, sanctification, deliverance, and authenticity.

1. Reverence. "Hallowed be thy name." Without properly acknowledging God's potential, disciple-makers cannot effectively win converts. Whenever believers carelessly downgrade God with expressions such as "the Man upstairs" and similar phraseology, God's otherness is minimized and human sinfulness becomes blurred. Anything that shrinks divine reality to human levels or elevates humanness to divine levels compromises humanity's need for God's forgiveness. Similarly, impersonal appellations for God distort God's personality, effectively portraying Him with "it" status rather than "He" significance. Since impersonal, nonreasoning forces cannot save us, the alternative becomes saving ourselves by maximizing the "light" (or "force") within. Essentially humans become their own saviors, while reverence protects us against this heresy.

2. Expectancy. "Your kingdom come." Halfhearted belief that distrusts God's ultimate power to fulfill His promises has emasculated the church's potency. Expressing our belief in God's unlimited power increases our belief. Jericho's walls might never have fallen had the Israelites not expressed their confidence by marching. Believers may honestly confess, "Help my unbelief," and heavenly assistance will strengthen our resolve. Vacillation, however, becomes the lethal injection that has destroyed many promising ministries. Indecisiveness regarding something as foundational as spiritual confidence can only generate failure. Ultimately, this means choosing between equivocation and expectancy. With certitude, Christ's kingdom comes and God's will prevails. The remaining question is, Where do you stand?

3. Surrender. "Your will be done." Whenever would-be soul winners live incompletely surrendered lives, their effectiveness is proportionately compromised. Televangelist Jimmy Swaggart's dalliance with prostitutes irreparably damaged his personal reputation and publicly humiliated Christianity. Ministers everywhere suffered the backlash. Subtler sins likewise have negative effects. Actually secretive sins sometimes produce greater negative results.

For example, a young couple outwardly expressed interest in evangelizing their neighbors and coworkers. They started studying the Bible with acquaintances on a regular schedule. The other couple confessed Christ, accepting Him as their Savior. They seriously considered joining the Christian fellowship that their mentors attended until vacationing with them in Chicago. The mentoring couples' use of anti-Semitic slurs revealed character defects that alienated the couple they had worked so diligently to reach. Complete surrender is the only alternative.

4. Dependence. "Give us this day." Wherever Christians demonstrate greater concern about bank accounts, retirement funds, and financial investments than they have for advancing God's kingdom, they tacitly say, "We're depending upon ourselves, our ingenuity, and our resourcefulness for survival." This compromises their witness. Matthew writes, "If God cares so wonderfully for wildflowers that are here today and thrown into the fire tomorrow, he will certainly care for you. . . . Don't worry about these things, saying, 'What will we eat? What will we drink?

What will we wear?' These things dominate the thoughts of unbelievers, but your heavenly Father already knows all your needs. Seek the Kingdom of God above all else. And live righteously, and he will give you everything you need" (Matthew 6:30–33, NLT).

5. *Confession and forgiveness.* "Forgive us." Until church members relinquish their self-righteousness, they cannot hope to convert lost souls. Romans 3:10, 23 depict the universal sinfulness of humankind. Pretenders who believe they are beyond temptation fool nobody except themselves. Unbelievers instinctively perceive this hypocrisy and become turned off. A believers' unforgiving condemnation of others likewise establishes roadblocks. Seeking divine forgiveness and offering personal forgiveness demonstrates the humility that gives Christian witness credibility. Without this disposition, little progress will transpire. Paul's abandonment of self-righteousness necessarily preceded his monumental accomplishments in soul winning. This remains true for all Christians.

6. *Sanctification and deliverance.* "Deliver us." Paul rhetorically asked, "Should we keep on sinning, so that God's wonderful kindness will show up even better?" (Romans 6:1, CEV). Paul answers with an emphatic negative! Forgiveness does not imply license. Sinning is forgivable but never acceptable. A sawdust trail revivalist once pitched his tabernacle among the inhabitants of a dreary frontier settlement. The mercantile and the saloon were the settlement's primary establishments. With little nighttime competition, the preacher's crusade was thronged nightly. One drunken visitor responded to his evangelistic appeal one evening. As he stumbled forward, someone shouted, "Don't baptize him preacher. He leaks!" Apparently, this was the eighth itinerant revivalist to visit that summer. Notwithstanding seven previous baptisms, the man was always intoxicated. Such inconsistencies call into question God's capabilities. Nonbelievers wonder why they should become Christians if nothing really happens. "Where's the difference?" they question. Wherever believers exhibit divine deliverance, other conversions follow.

7. *Authenticity.* "Use not vain repetitions." Christ warned against the hypocrisy of those Pharisees who offered ostentatious prayers. Their counterfeit piousness tarnished the reputations of true believers. Their religious display fooled nobody except themselves. Jesus counseled His followers to do otherwise. Pray privately. But Christ's concern was not privacy. Daniel prayed publicly and doing otherwise would have compromised his witness. Praying to impress people, however, angered Jesus.

Discipleship

Genuine Christians communicate with their heavenly Father for soul nourishment, not human adulation. Oftentimes public prayer is warranted. Believers can conscientiously pray openly whenever properly motivated. However, no adequate substitution has been found for private prayer.

Jesus selected followers and matched them with responsibilities commensurate with their capabilities. He patiently trained them, utilizing small groups and face-to-face communication. He emphasized personal experience governed by scriptural messages and efficacious prayer. He cultivated industriousness. These formed the building blocks for spiritual leadership.

CHAPTER 12

Healthy creatures reproduce themselves. The previous chapter outlined what Jesus emphasized in maintaining His disciples' spiritual health. Were they, indeed, healthy? If so, they were prepared for spiritual reproduction; if not, Christian extinction would have transpired within a generation. Christ's further instruction and patterning (advanced spiritual leadership) prepared these chosen disciples for spiritual propagation. *Propagation* is an interesting word associated with reproduction, proliferation, and procreation. Otherwise stated, propagation is breeding. We also associate it with broadcasting, dissemination, and transmission. These form appropriate connections that help us understand God's design for making additional disciples.

Biological reproduction seldom occurs without physical intimacy. Exceptions happen through artificial means. These occurrences, however, necessitate exorbitant financial outlays and sometimes involve risky procedures. God's natural old-fashioned approach is inexpensive, intuitive, and pleasurable. Who needs *inexpensive* explained? *Intuitive* signifies knowing something instinctively, automatically, or unconsciously. *Pleasurable* means enjoyable, doing something you relish.

Spiritual reproduction seldom occurs without spiritual intimacy. Sometimes exceptions happen through artificial means: telecommunications, computers, media blitzes, Christian magazine subscriptions, and so on. These occurrences, however, necessitate exorbitant financial outlays and sometimes involve questionable procedures and methodologies. God's natural old-fashioned approach is inexpensive, intuitive, and pleasurable.

Inexpensive

Quality television cameras often exceed the sticker price of new automobiles. Additional equipment includes mixers, microphones, speakers, and so on, nothing cheap. Will cost-ineffective telecommunications bridge the spiritual reproduction gap? Have humans lost the personal touch? What was your last billing statement for laughing with your neighbor? What was your last payment for gardening with friends? Have you declared bankruptcy because you shared recipes across the fence?

Intuitive

How many men have taken classes about how to ask women out? How many dissertations have you written or published about that subject? Did you spend countless hours rehearsing your pick-up lines? Nothing intuitive about that! Nevertheless, churches everywhere offer formalized instruction, oftentimes called witnessing classes, in which Christians rehearse their spiritual pick-up lines but seldom use them. When I first met my wife, I had no preprepared speeches, rehearsed pick-up lines, or formalized dating training. Everything happened rather intuitively.

Pleasurable

Imagine cultivating a courtship by saying, "You'll have to date, otherwise your parents will disown you. You should be ashamed about not having an interest in dating. If you love your parents, you'll date. Your nanny will be offering dating classes for the next eight weeks and you'll attend unless you don't like dating. The person who doesn't like dating, doesn't get married, and doesn't have children, will lose his or her inheritance." Does dating, expressed like this, sound *pleasurable*? Explain, then, why churches utilize shame, guilt, and fear to promote witnessing. Spiritual intimacy is pleasurable. Making kingdom friends, also known as disciples, is enjoyable.

Youthful energy may be directed effectively into disciple-making. Eventually, this will become intuitive. Remember, disciple-making is not merely being neighborly. Many worthwhile service projects are organized through churches and youth organizations. Christian service is invaluable and inculcates meaningful aspects of model citizenship. Mistaking it for disciple-making, however, would be perilous. Christ's commission was not, "Therefore enter the entire world raking leaves and painting fences." Jesus' declaration was, instead, "Therefore enter the world and make disciples." Youth are young only once. Teaching them service is important. Completing their experience with passionately modeled disciple-making is *nonnegotiable*. Raking leaves and painting fences have opened callous hearts for Christ, but our mission is not accomplished until spiritual commitments have been secured. Omitting the disciple-making aspects will effectively cripple their adult witness. Wherever young people have experienced authentic disciple-making during youth, their adult witness has happened intuitively.

Would expensive evangelistic crusades be deemed necessary, wherever significant numbers of believers live, if those Christians found witnessing pleasurable and intuitive? Large-scale preaching venues *are* biblical and crusades could spearhead Christian proclamation wherever no churches exist. They might constitute meaningful adjuncts to Christians' intuitive daily ministry. But they have largely become substitutes for personal witnessing and disciple-making. Believers have surrendered their spiritual reproductive rights to religious professionals.

Finding little pleasure through disciple-making and lacking those foundational experiences that transform disciple-making practices into intuitive lifestyles, congregations that even bother thinking about disciple-making have resorted to financing "professionals." Guilt produces strange partnerships. This unholy alliance brings guilt-ridden church attendees together with clergypersons who willingly accept the responsibility for disciple-making and congregation building.

Unfortunately, these ministers are overpaid. One nineteenth-century observer noted a crew foreman who was vigorously digging while several crew members stood idly watching. Upon discovering this, their employer immediately fired the foreman. The foreman felt disrespected because he was working harder than anyone. The employer explained he could not afford paying foreman's wages for one person's common labor while everyone else watched unproductively. Foremen are tasked with employing the capabilities of their entire crew. Their chief responsibility is empowering them for mission achievement, not achieving the mission themselves. Ministers are likewise tasked with employing the capabilities of their entire congregation for accomplishing the divinely ordained mission of extending God's kingdom through disciple-making. When empowerment is correctly executed, expensive outlays become unnecessary.

Those resources are then effectively redirected to areas wherever the gospel is unheard and believers are nonexistent or small in numbers.

How did the Master Disciple-Maker hand down this legacy? First, Christ fostered a rejoicing culture. Pleasurability and enjoyment were highlighted rather than disdained. The very anticipation of Jesus' arrival created happiness. Speaking about the Magi, Matthew writes, "When they saw the star [which revealed the Messiah's location], they were overjoyed" (Matthew 2:10, NIV). Pleasure begins within God's presence. Rejoicing multiplies whenever another person enters that presence. Although Christ encourages this joyfulness throughout His ministry, Luke offers the quintessential portrait of rejoicing through three short parables.

> Then Jesus told them this parable: "Suppose one of you has a hundred sheep and loses one of them. Doesn't he leave the ninety-nine in the open country and go after the lost sheep until he finds it? And when he finds it, he joyfully puts it on his shoulders and goes home. Then he calls his friends and neighbors together and says, 'Rejoice with me; I have found my lost sheep.' I tell you that in the same way there will be more rejoicing in heaven over one sinner who repents than over ninety-nine righteous persons who do not need to repent.
>
> "Or suppose a woman has ten silver coins and loses one. Doesn't she light a lamp, sweep the house and search carefully until she finds it? And when she finds it, she calls her friends and neighbors together and says, 'Rejoice with me; I have found my lost coin.' In the same way, I tell you, there is rejoicing in the presence of the angels of God over one sinner who repents" (Luke 15:3–10, NIV).

The most powerful parable Jesus saves for last: the prodigal son. This philanderer squanders his inheritance on drunkenness and prostitution. Finally bankrupt, the errant child returns to his wounded father and begs for mercy. Rather than reprimanding or humiliating the penitent, the father offers his finest clothing and throws a barbeque! " 'Bring the fattened calf and kill it. Let's have a feast and celebrate. For this son of mine was dead and is alive again; he was lost and is found.' So they began to celebrate" (verses 23, 24, NIV).

Not only did Christ establish a culture of pleasurableness, He, secondly, actively engaged His followers with assignments designed for involvement in ministry. Luke 10 records,

> The Lord now chose seventy-two other disciples and sent them ahead in pairs to all the towns and places he planned to visit. . . .
>
> When the seventy-two disciples returned, they joyfully reported to him, "Lord, even the demons obey us when we use your name!" (verses 1, 17, NLT).

Can we help but recognize their overwhelming excitement? On the author's sixth Christmas, weeks of anticipation culminated in the opening of the oversized cardboard carton secured behind the tree. Great rejoicing followed as Father mounted wheels and handlebars on that scarlet J. C. Higgins bicycle. The following weeks were filled with wonderful father-son moments—instruction, demonstration, falling, more instruction, demonstration, and falling—until the mission of bicycle riding was mastered. Sharing that accomplishment with his father was one of the proudest moments of that six-year-old's life. Watching others ride bicycles might provide limited enjoyment, but nothing in comparison with the thrills derived from riding oneself. Christ actively engaged His disciples in pleasurable ministry.

Does your church's culture celebrate redemption? Does it highlight disciple-making? Does disciple-making form the centerpiece of your church's ministry or is Christian growth relegated to that unending list of church activities—building projects, church picnics, board sessions, planning committees, "sanctified" gossiping, and more committees? Are baptisms and accessions opportunities for celebration or bothersome routines that must be fitted around more "important" matters? Instead, does your church culture prioritize Christian growth? Are baptisms and welcoming new members into God's family given preference in church life and the worship services? Is this center stage or item number twenty-seven on somebody's list?

Imagine a soccer team that never celebrated their goals, giving priority to advertising, stadium concession booths, parking matters, broadcasting the matches, and uniform designs instead. Assume that goals were unimportant peripherals in that team's corporate culture. Financial considerations, public relations, and network contracts trumped scoring goals and winning matches. Professional athletics has become a supersized business; winning, however, still measures success: outscoring opponents still produces wins. Winning franchises satisfy their audiences while losing franchises lose theirs. Winning franchises peddle more merchandise, witness greater attendance (thereby increasing concession income), and attract lucrative broadcasting contracts. Celebrating incoming disciples becomes first priority among healthy churches. Everything else becomes secondary. This attitude should be intuitive in all healthy churches.

Jesus cultivated intuitive disciple-making through His personal example. Intuitive disciple-making is (1) untethered, that is, unfastened from canned speeches, proselytizing formulas, and rigid methodologies; (2) phosphorescent, that is, light emitting following exposure to a stimulating source (Jesus!); and (3) spontaneous, that is, unrehearsed, flowing freely from the Holy Spirit's leadership within our hearts.

Christian disciples are delusional whenever they think that there are prepared answers for every seeker's question. There are appropriate times for remonstrance and apologetics (defending Christian faith against philosophical attacks). None, however, should withdraw from personal witnessing because they have not memorized forceful arguments nor studied philosophy. Some misguided teachers have adopted that faulty approach, which suggests that disciple-making means answering every intellectual objection to faith. Their training methodology consists of memorizing arguments against these objections. Frequently, their followers exude an intellectual arrogance or spiritual snobbery. Jesus, however, looked for spokespersons, not robots. Christ admonished,

> "They will hand you over to the courts and scourge you in their synagogues; and you will even be brought before govenors and kings for My sake, as a testimony to them and to the Gentiles. But when they hand you over, do not worry about how or what you are to say; for it will be given you in that hour what you are to say. For it is not you who speak, but it is the Spirit of your Father who speaks in you" (Matthew 10:17–20, NASB).

Believers are untethered from self-dependence, released for the Holy Spirit's exclusive leadership. Wherever Christians have depended upon their methodologies instead of the Holy Spirit, aberrations have occurred and Christian witness has suffered.

Intuitive discipleship is likewise phosphorescent. Christ's disciples emit light whenever they have been exposed to Jesus. They automatically supply hopefulness to those they contact. Like Paul's associate, Barnabas, they naturally encourage others. They stimulate the worthiest characteristics of others. Jesus modeled this repeatedly. Christ's disciples devalued children; Jesus befriended them. These disciples likewise scorned the Samaritan woman; Christ inspired her. Christ's closest associates despised people like Zacchaeus; Jesus embraced social misfits. Intuitive disciples derive spiritual energy from Christ's fellowship, then they brighten their world, emitting peacefulness, acceptance, compassion, security, and joyfulness.

The foundation of this attitude is not manipulative methodologies designed to "hook" new believers by making Christianity appear attractive. These attitudes are not superficial coverings donned for appearance's sake but later relinquished. This outlook represents fundamental values, rooted in divine grace, which transform planet Earth.

Finally, intuitive discipleship is spontaneous. It is not guilt driven: "If I don't distribute twenty tracts every week, God will hold me accountable for millions destroyed by everlasting fire!" It is not anxiety ridden: "What if the Holy Spirit directs me to someone and I miss it?" It is not shame driven: "The preacher says we're the slowest-growing congregation of our entire region and we're really looking bad." It is not self-conscious: "I keep disordering the twelve spiritual laws and the four steps and can't remember the cosmological argument for God's existence." These are external concerns or influences. Spontaneity arises from within.

Spontaneous disciples keep spiritual matters central. They construct life around Christ and the Holy Spirit. Christ cultivated this characteristic via modeling. Jesus constructed His life around His Father's through prayer, familiarity with Scripture (including memorization), and significant exposure to natural wonders. He did not make disciples to prove something (external motivation) but because overflowing compassion naturally expressed itself through wanting the unsurpassed life for others (internal motivation). As volcanoes naturally release the fire within themselves, so spontaneous Christians naturally release the spiritual enthusiasm within themselves.

Jesus modeled and taught pleasurable and intuitive disciple-making. Those teachings and experiences should establish the guidelines for Christian outreach today. Two thousand years ago, Jesus removed the fear and restored the joy of disciple-making. What He did for Matthew, Thaddeus, and Andrew then, He can do for you now.

CHAPTER 13

David's self-confidence was presently being rewarded. To evaluate his military strength, he rebelliously initiated a census that even worldly Joab disapproved. David's actions indicated self-dependence rather than divine reliance, and heavenly accountability followed. David selected from three potential punitive measures, choosing three days of plagues. Devastation followed as David desperately sought to arrest the plagues. The prophetic directive was to establish an altar at the Jebusite Araunah's threshing floor. David hastily approached Araunah, pleading to purchase the designated property. The dedicated subject willingly offered his monarch the property without charge plus the required sacrificial offerings. David responded, "I won't offer the Lord my God burnt sacrifices that cost me nothing" (2 Samuel 24:24, God's Word).

Although costly, those sacrifices were not meritorious. They merely indicated David's relinquishment of self-confidence and resultant humility. Generations later, Christ would declare, "When you've done everything you're ordered to do, say, 'We're worthless servants. We've only done our duty' " (Luke 17:10, God's Word). These concepts frame our exploration of costly discipleship.

Christian discipleship costs. Discipleship is priceless but also costly. Anyone who desires smooth highways, luxurious trappings, and stress-free living must look elsewhere. Neither do genuine disciples expect adulation for merely carrying forth their assignments. Such applause denigrates discipleship. Their humility surrenders everything—applause, praise, commendation—to their King.

Jesus says,

> "If you want to be my disciple, you must hate everyone else by comparison—your father and mother, wife and children, brothers and sisters—yes, even your own life. Otherwise you cannot be my disciple. And if you do not carry your own cross and follow me, you cannot be my disciple.
>
> "But don't begin until you count the cost. For who would begin construction of a building without first calculating the cost to see if there is enough money to finish it? Otherwise, you might complete only the foundation before running out of money, and then everyone would laugh at you. They would say, 'There's the person who started the building and couldn't afford to finish it!'
>
> "Or what king would go to war against another king without first sitting down with his counselors to discuss whether his army of 10,000 could defeat the 20,000 soldiers marching against him? And if he can't, he will send a delegation to discuss terms of peace while the enemy is still far away. So you cannot become my disciple without giving up everything you own" (Luke 14:26–33, NLT).

What is involved?

"You must hate everyone." What incomprehensible words from our *loving* Savior. Their offensiveness can hardly be overlooked, even when considered hyperbolic. Jewish society cherished, protected, and honored their elderly citizens. More than mere neighborliness, their spiritual obligation was anchored in Moses' commandments. Teachers were treated respectfully, even affectionately, but, scripturally speaking, only God deserved such uncompromising devotion as Christ demanded. Matthew's parallel in Matthew 10:37 softens this offensiveness somewhat, approximately rephrasing the reading to "loving less," but Christ unquestionably expected undivided commitment. Valuing Christ above family approval was nonnegotiable. Hardly could stronger wording have been selected.

Gwendolyn Schmachtenberg* was raised by adoring parents who fellowshiped with other Christians in a historical European-based

---

* A pseudonym.

denomination. Opulent ritualism characterized their worship. Exclusivity characterized their worldview. Intermarriage with nonbelievers, meaning everyone outside their denomination, was explicitly forbidden. Other denominations were neither countenanced nor acknowledged. Gwendolyn deeply appreciated her upbringing. Nevertheless, spiritually yearning for something beyond her ritualistic religious background, she began exploring other religions. She discovered another Christian fellowship that was scripturally centered and relationally focused. Cultivating a personal relationship with God, experiencing complete forgiveness exclusively through divine grace, and living obediently through spiritual transformation rather than anxiety-driven external motivations intrigued Gwendolyn. Conscientiously, she sensed that God's providence was leading her towards scripturally based faith rather than ritualistically based experience. Integrity prevailed and she started worshiping with the Bible-based fellowship rather than with her traditional church.

This defection scandalized her relatives. Rejection followed. Gwendolyn's mother, particularly, disavowed her altogether. Having relinquished her childhood religion, she was effectively expelled by her family. Miss Schmachtenberg afterwards married someone from that Christian fellowship through which her spiritual experience had been transformed. When he subsequently abandoned her and their four children, she experienced little family support.

Conscientious Christian discipleship is priceless but costly. Following Jesus is spiritually enriching, but oftentimes materially impoverishing. Gwendolyn's discipleship cost her the closeness she once had with her family, and she lost the financial support she possibly would have received during her marital crisis. Putting Christ's calling above family approval will never be painless but will always be required. Such narratives are endless; yet, these sacrifices allow Christ fresh opportunities to encourage and nourish believers' faith.

"Hate . . . yes, even your own life." Christ does not encourage here some schizophrenic disorder whereby self-abhorrence is cultivated. Jesus does, however, stipulate that prioritization whereby God is elevated and humanity humbled. Humility and humiliation are linguistically related but significantly different. Humility in this context signifies that willingness, internally motivated, through which individuals acknowledge their Creator and worship their Maker rather than self. Humiliation signifies involuntarily having one's personal reputation damaged. Humility signifies

heartfelt offering, humiliation, and begrudged embarrassment.

David was humble; Saul was humiliated. Humility indicates attitudes whereby believers sacrifice personal opinions, sublimate egotistical self-perceptions, and temper personal aspirations for God's kingdom advancement. Throughout history there are numerous examples wherein this verse was more literally interpreted, meaning that believers sacrificed their lives under Christ's sovereignty.

American legendary patriot Nathan Hale once declared, "I regret that I have but one life to give for my country." That assertiveness reverberates throughout Christian biographies.

> But others were tortured, refusing to turn from God in order to be set free. They placed their hope in a better life after the resurrection. Some were jeered at, and their backs were cut open with whips. Others were chained in prisons. Some died by stoning, some were sawed in half, and others were killed with the sword. Some went about wearing skins of sheep and goats, destitute and oppressed and mistreated. They were too good for this world, wandering over deserts and mountains, hiding in caves and holes in the ground (Hebrews 11:35–38, NLT).

John Hus, and subsequently his disciple Jerome, suffered burning at the stake. Eventually, exciting King Henry VIII's wrath for public opposition against his divorce of Catherine, Tyndale was arrested in Antwerp and imprisoned in Vilvoorde castle, near Brussels, for eighteen months. Authorities proffered advocates and procurators (legal defense attorneys), which Tyndale refused, instead defending himself. Rather than begrudging his miserable circumstances and questioning God's providence, Tyndale, shadowing Paul's ancient example, taught whoever would listen, ultimately converting his jailer, his jailer's daughter, and several members of the jailer's household. Impressed by Tyndale's sincerity, Christian comportment, and comprehensible instruction, others exclaimed that if Tyndale was not an exemplary Christian, they did not know anyone who was. Around October 1536, during the Augsburg assembly, the emperor decreed Tyndale's execution. He perished by strangulation, the hangman afterwards igniting that conflagration that consumed his body.

Jim Elliot's character was revealed years before his martyrdom. High school classmates recount how Elliot quoted Scripture to the student body president and then explained his refusal to attend their class party. Elsewhere he jeopardized his standing with the public-speaking club, refusing to contribute a political speech because of personal convictions that Christians should avoid political involvement. Elliot's speaking capabilities and theatrical successes caused some high school teachers to encourage an entertainment career. Mirroring Moses, who "refused to be called the son of Pharaoh's daughter, preferring to suffer hardship with the people of God rather than enjoy the transient pleasures of sin" (Hebrews 11:24, 25, NEB), Elliot dedicated himself to mission service. He unapologetically defended his mediocre college grades in classes such as anthropology, politics, and philosophy, saying that studying Scripture was more important. He strongly believed in physical conditioning and self-discipline, joining the wrestling team. Violence, however, was anathema; Elliot purposed that should he be drafted, he would register as a conscientious objector. These principles and experiences formed the spiritual foundation for his short-lived missionary service.

Speaking with Brazilian missionaries at the International Student Missionary Convention, Elliot became convicted that God was leading him into Central American tribal missions. Four missionary families launched their outreach for the primitive Huaorani tribesmen from Shandia Mission Station, Ecuador. Although possessing firearms, the men had covenanted not to defend themselves against Huaorani attacks. They reasoned that their salvation was secured, but ending the tribesmen's lives would terminate their opportunity for redemption. On January 8, 1956, Huaorani tribesmen attacked Elliot's group, killing five of them.

The names Elliot, McCully, Fleming, Youderian, and Saint were forever engraved into the consciousness of American missionary enterprise. Elliot never witnessed his daughter's first birthday. McCully perished before his youngest son's birth. Nine innocent children were deprived of their fathers. More than six years beforehand Elliot had recorded the following journal entry: "He is no fool who gives what he cannot keep to gain that which he cannot lose." Five young disciples in their late twenties and early thirties forfeited their futures, their families, and their dreams for reasons misunderstood by nonbelievers: they believed their gospel commissioning more sacred than life itself. They counted the cost, paying the ultimate price.

That price is not always martyrdom. Sometimes living can inflict more punishment than dying. Amy Wilson Carmichael, born December 16, 1867, in Millisle, Ireland, was the eldest of seven children. Like Jim Elliot, her character was shaped early by devout Christian parents. Mischievous beyond description, Carmichael no doubt tantalized her younger siblings by her daring but probably scandalized her proper Presbyterian parents. Her behavior undoubtedly played some role in dismissing so many governesses except one she loved: Eleanor Milne. Milne's narrative repertoire included the religious martyrdoms of great Scottish and English figures such as Nicholas Ridley and Hugh Latimer, who were executed together. Ridley encouraged Latimer, saying, "Be of good heart, brother, for God will either assuage the fury of the flame, or else strengthen us to abide it." After the conflagration was kindled Latimer responded, "Be of good comfort, Master Ridley, and play the man. We shall this day light such a candle by God's grace in England as I trust shall never be put out."

Another early experience became her turning point. Returning from church, her family encountered an elderly woman dragging a heavy bundle. The children assisted her but experienced great embarrassment, fearing that other respectable people returning from church services would assume they were homeless waifs themselves. While passing an ornate Victorian fountain, Paul's words suddenly flashed before Carmichael's mind:

> Gold, silver, precious stones, hay, stubble; every man's work shall be made manifest: for the day shall declare it, because it shall be revealed by fire; and the fire shall try every man's work of what sort it is. If any man's work abide which he hath built thereupon, he shall receive a reward (1 Corinthians 3:12–14, KJV).

The impression was so startling that Carmichael turned unsuccessfully to find the speaker.

Following that incident she became involved with the Belfast City Mission ministering to poorer children. She initiated weekly prayer meetings for school girls at Victoria College and taught "shawlies," mill girls who donned inexpensive shawls rather than unaffordable hats, at the Rosemary Street Presbyterian Church. In 1887, she heard Hudson Taylor, the China Inland Mission's founder, at the Keswick Convention, and she became convinced of her missionary calling. She was prepared for departure under the auspices of China Inland Mission when doctors decided that her health failed their standards (she suffered from neuralgia). The physician's decision notwithstanding, Carmichael determined to follow her calling. Finding assistance from the Church Missionary Society, she sailed for Japan, later serving Ceylon before settling in Dohnavur, India, where she spent fifty-three years rescuing young children from abuse and prostitution.

During those years (she never took a furlough), she received a letter from some young inquirer who was considering missionary service. She asked what missionary life was like. Carmichael responded, "Missionary life is simply a chance to die." Without regrets Amy Carmichael had counted the cost—physical deprivation, lifelong emotional separation from family, potentially violent confrontations with child abusers—and paid the price. Discipleship is priceless but not cheap.

"Carry your own cross and follow me." Christ projects forward through these verses to His upcoming crucifixion. Condemned criminals who lugged their crosses to Golgotha were often met by jeering crowds. Denigration, exhaustion, hopelessness, betrayal, and ingratitude all characterized the crucifixion experience. Ironically, that disgusting symbol of shame, immortalized as "The Old Rugged Cross," has been gold-plated, silver-plated, bronzed, and diamond-studded until costly discipleship and cross-bearing are long-forgotten relics of long-lost devotion. "The Contemporized Smoothed Cross" has reconstructed worship, fellowship, and discipleship. Worship has become entertainment, fellowship has morphed into meaningless activities, and discipleship has simply disappeared.

Still within the recesses of human personality irrepressible longings for the cross experience exist. Does this signify a masochistic yearning for denigration, exhaustion, hopelessness, betrayal, and ingratitude? Hardly. These negative associations happened because of human sinfulness. Our hearts yearn for the character that declares, "Slander my reputation, ridicule my compassion, lampoon my spirituality, caricature my religion, attack my family with vituperative epithets, and otherwise establish the righteousness of my cause. I cannot be moved!" Cross-bearing Christians do not yearn for persecution but possess characters that refuse to compromise integrity, willingly accepting persecution rather than forfeiting truth.

Desmond Doss entered the armed services, willing to serve but unwilling to kill. The misunderstood draftee was frequently subjected to verbal abuse. His religion was ridiculed, his girlfriend's reputation was besmirched, his praying lampooned, and his unwillingness to kill equated with cowardice. Fellow soldiers threatened his life. The army nearly dismissed him from military service. Doss, however, would neither shortchange his religious faith nor abandon his patriotic ideals. He accepted his castigation as the cross he bore for his faithfulness to God.

During combat, however, he repeatedly proved himself, saving hundreds of lives while endangering his own. In Okinawa alone, he rescued seventy-five soldiers in one operation. Those who had ridiculed him embraced his selfless character and seemingly inexhaustible strength. One commander even postponed an engagement so that Doss could complete his daily Bible reading. Desmond Thomas Doss, the seemingly insignificant Virginian, was awarded three Purple Hearts, two Bronze Stars, and the highest military honor conferred by the United States of America, the Medal of Honor. Although never alone, he carried his cross. He paid the price.

"Giving up everything you own." Deep-seated grief chiseled his countenance. His self-assured manner was melting, being presently replaced by incalculable angst. His expectations were being shattered. This Nazarene demanded everything. The grieving visitor wrestled with this expectation. All things considered, he lived respectably, more righteously than many contemporaries. God's commandments had been honored, treating his parents honorably, refraining from adultery, murder, embezzlement, and dishonesty. Neighbors respected, even liked, this wealthy youthful magistrate. Why was this unacceptable? Why was more required? Why did the Rabbi answer, "Sell *all*"? Tithing (10 percent of one's income) would have worked. Perhaps even 50 percent (overly generous but possible) would have worked. The Scriptures had never even required that much.

Should he abandon everything he and his ancestors had worked to achieve? How would his family survive? What would their neighbors, friends, and associates think? Why should his family be subjected to the embarrassment of being confused with paupers when they owned so much? Their estate was extensive. Why did Jesus the Messiah demand everything? Scripture records that he sorrowfully spurned Christ's invitation (Matthew 19:16–22). The invitation is priceless. The cost is everything.

Robert LeTourneau eschewed formal education during his youth. He traveled through several jobs, becoming especially interested in earth-moving equipment. His welding skills, earthmoving experience, and innate mechanical inclination combined to create the greatest manufacturer of earthmoving equipment. During the Second World War, his earthmoving equipment and engineering vehicles represented 70 percent of the machinery utilized by American forces. He claimed responsibility for nearly three hundred patents.

These notable accomplishments, however, were dwarfed by his Christian commitment. He gained fame for his philanthropy. Eventually, he started and funded a Christian university, enabled numerous mission projects, and reportedly invested 90 percent of his income in Christian work while living on the remaining 10 percent. Many Christians, perhaps most, complain about returning 10 percent to God while living on 90 percent. LeTourneau, a phenomenal businessman, realized his contributions were actually heavenly investments. He recognized that nothing multiplied like heavenly investments, thus sinking *everything* he owned into Christ. The invitation is priceless. The cost is everything. The investment is out of this world.

"Count the cost." Now the decision is yours. You can invest your energies in earthly stocks, thus living for momentary pleasures and materialistic achievements. The game Monopoly captures this microcosmically. Contestants purchase properties, buildings, transportation, and other commodities battling for monopoly of the board. After everyone is absolutely tired out, somebody triumphs and the diversion stops. Winner and losers alike replace their buildings and properties in the game's box and shelve it. In reality, funeral directors place winners and losers in boxes, burying them, while their properties, toys, and buildings get restocked for someone else to contest. The triumph is temporal, quickly disappearing, and the contest concludes with no enduring real estate, no eternal mansions, and worms for roommates.

This choice, historically, constitutes the most preferred selection. Others, nonetheless, have selected preferred heavenly stocks and have spent their lives spreading God's Word, preparing committed Christian disciples, and hastening His return. Unlike the Monopoly option, this offers enduring real estate; mansions that will not rust, rot, or tarnish; and angels for roommates. Our co-investors have been fusillade targets, human torches, and torture victims. More commonly they have been ridiculed students, forsaken relatives, misunderstood employees, and rejected outsiders. They will awaken someday with those who became Christ's disciples through their efforts. With Paul, they exclaim,

> Finally, there is laid up for me the crown of righteousness, which the Lord, the righteous Judge, will give to me on that Day, and not to me only but also to all who have loved His appearing (2 Timothy 4:8).

This much Christ expects: nothing more, nothing less, nothing else. They have counted the cost.

Have you?

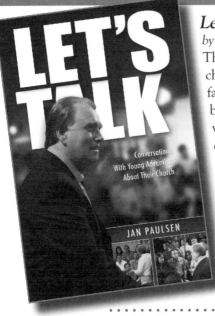